Welcome, Kids!

Are you ready for some fun? We're going to visit America's national parks. Do you know there are over 400 parks? That's a lot. But we've organized them into geographic regions—nine regions in all.

In this book you'll find a map for each region with the parks listed. You'll learn what's special about them. And you'll learn about the interesting stories they tell. These stories have been grouped into themes that help explain why these special places have been set aside to be protected and enjoyed. We've added activities for each region so you and your family can learn even more about the parks.

Of course, the most fun comes when you visit the parks yourself. This book gives you tips on things to look for and a place to record your visits and the names of the park rangers you meet.

So, grab your pencil and crayons and let's get started. You'll find answers to the activities at the end of the book. If you have a computer, you can dig even deeper as you start a lifetime adventure discovering America's national parks.

The geographic regions in this book match those found in the *Passport To Your National Parks®* book. To collect the cancellation stamps for page 40 and the inside back cover, visit the Passport cancellation station usually found at the park's visitor center. For more information about the Passport program visit **ShopANP.org**

To learn more about our national parks visit **nps.gov**

You can be a Junior Ranger even if you are not able to visit a national park. Visit **nps.gov/kids/become-a-junior-ranger.htm** for information.

9 National Park Regions of the United States

- **North Atlantic Region** — Pages 4-6
  - Theme: Revolutionary War — Page 7
- **Mid-Atlantic Region** — Pages 8-10
  - Theme: Civil War — Page 11
- **National Capital Region** — Pages 12-14
  - Theme: Presidents — Page 15
- **Southeast Region** — Pages 16-18
  - Theme: African American History — Page 19
- **Midwest Region** — Pages 20-22
  - Theme: Famous Americans — Page 23
- **Southwest Region** — Pages 24-26
  - Theme: Westward Expansion — Page 27
- **Rocky Mountain Region** — Pages 28-30
  - Theme: Nature's Wonders — Page 31
- **Western Region** — Pages 32-34
  - Theme: Seashores & Lakeshores — Page 35
- **Pacific Northwest & Alaska Region** — Pages 36-38
  - Theme: Recreational Sites — Page 39

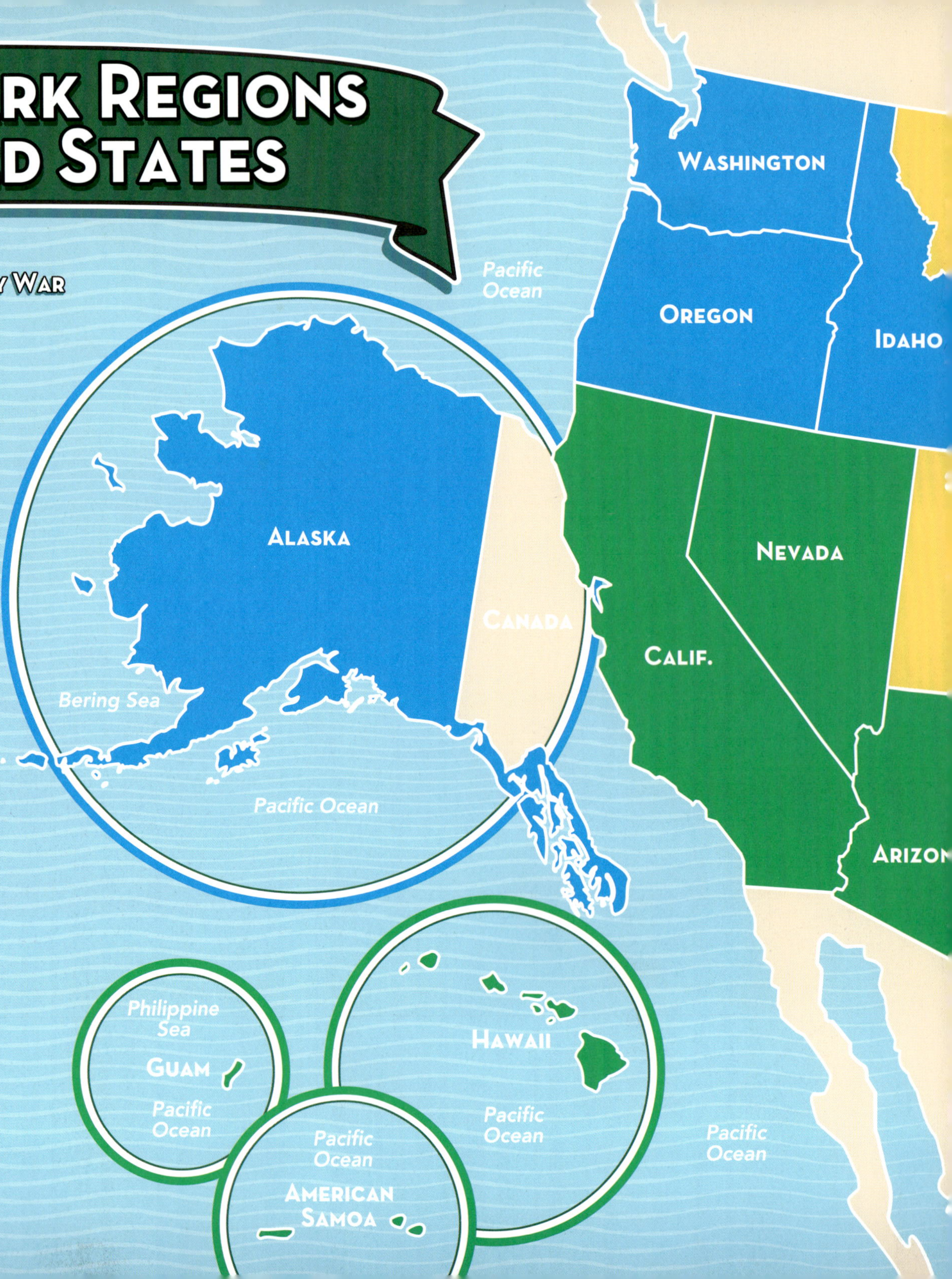

Canada
Montana
North Dakota
South Dakota
Wyoming
Utah
Colorado
Minn.
Wisconsin
Mich.
Michigan
Iowa
Nebraska
Kansas
Missouri
Illinois
Ind.
Ohio
Maine
Vt.
N.H.
Mass.
R.I.
Conn.
New York
N.J.
Pennsylvania
Md.
Del.
W. Va.
Virginia
Washington, D.C.
Kentucky
Tennessee
North Carolina
South Carolina
Oklahoma
Arkansas
New Mexico
Texas
Louisiana
Miss.
Ala.
Georgia
Fla.
Atlantic Ocean
Gulf of Mexico
Mexico
Atlantic Ocean
Puerto Rico
Virgin Islands
Caribbean Sea

North Atlantic Region

Statue of Liberty

Maze of Liberty
Can you find your way to the top of Lady Liberty?

End Here

Start Here

National Parks in the North Atlantic Region

You don't have to go far to find a national park in the North Atlantic Region. Nearly half of the region's parks are in Boston and New York; others are in forested or rural areas or along the Atlantic Coast.

These parks offer a wonderful variety of things to see and do. Learn about early French explorers at Saint Croix Island IHS. At Saugus Iron Works NHS, see how iron was made for tools to build colonial homes. Walk the decks of historic vessels at Salem Maritime NHS and New Bedford Whaling NHP. Visit the homes of four U.S. presidents and the only national site dedicated to a first lady. As the birthplace of the nation, this region is also rich with Revolutionary War sites.

There's more than history to discover here—like swimming and exploring the beaches at Cape Cod and Fire Island national seashores and looking for wildlife along the trails at Acadia NP.

From building your own wooden fort at Fort Stanwix to camping out under the stars on one of the Boston Harbor Islands, you'll enjoy this region's varied parks.

Did You Know?

- It takes 354 steps to walk up to the crown of the Statue of Liberty.

- Teddy bears are named for President Theodore Roosevelt, who was born in New York. Although stories differ on who made the first of these popular stuffed toys, there is little doubt that they were named for the president in 1902 or 1903.

- Acadia NP is so far east that you can stand on Cadillac Mountain and be one of the first persons in the U.S. to see the sun rise.

- Silversmith Paul Revere was also a dentist. He wired individual false teeth for people—made from hippopotamus teeth!

- The Minute Men of New England got their name because they could be ready to fight in a minute. Their weapons were always nearby, and they were as well trained as any American soldiers who fought in the American Revolutionary War.

- The house where poet Henry Wadsworth Longfellow lived from 1837 to 1882 served as one of George Washington's headquarters during the American Revolution. You can see it at Longfellow House – Washington's Headquarters NHS.

Acadia National Park

MAINE
- Appalachian NST (from ME to GA)
- Katahdin Woods and Waters NM
- Saint Croix Island IHS
- Acadia NP
- ★ AUGUSTA

Moose: *I'm rarely found in the East now, but look for me at Acadia National Park.*

VERMONT
- ★ MONTPELIER
- Marsh-Billings-Rockefeller NHP

N.H.
- ★ CONCORD
- Saint-Gaudens NHP

NEW YORK
- Saratoga NHP
- Fort Stanwix NM
- Harriet Tubman NHP
- ★ ALBANY
- Martin Van Buren NHS
- Women's Rights NHP
- Theodore Roosevelt Inaugural NHS
- Vanderbilt Mansion NHS
- Eleanor Roosevelt NHS
- Home of Franklin D. Roosevelt NHS

MASS.
- Lowell NHP
- Blackstone River Valley NHP
- Springfield Armory NHS
- ★ BOSTON

BOSTON AREA:
- Adams NHP
- Boston NHP
- Boston African American NHS
- Boston Harbor Islands NRA
- Frederick Law Olmsted NHS
- John Fitzgerald Kennedy NHS
- Longfellow House–Washington's Headquarters NHS
- Minute Man NHP
- Salem Maritime NHS
- Saugus Iron Works NHS

- Cape Cod NS
- Roger Williams N MEM
- ★ PROVIDENCE
- **R.I.**
- New Bedford Whaling NHP

CONN.
- ★ HARTFORD
- Weir Farm NHP
- Sagamore Hill NHS
- Fire Island NS
- NEW YORK CITY

NEW YORK CITY AREA:
- African Burial Ground NM
- Castle Clinton NM
- Federal Hall N MEM
- Gateway NRA (also N.J.)
- General Grant N MEM
- Governors Island NM
- Hamilton Grange N MEM
- Saint Paul's Church NHS
- Statue of Liberty NM
- Stonewall NM
- Theodore Roosevelt Birthplace NHS

Elizabeth Cady Stanton: *I was a women's rights leader in the late 1800s. You can learn about me at Women's Rights NHP.*

Paul Revere: *You can learn about my famous midnight ride at Boston National Historical Park.*

BROWN — Color in the circles of the parks you visit

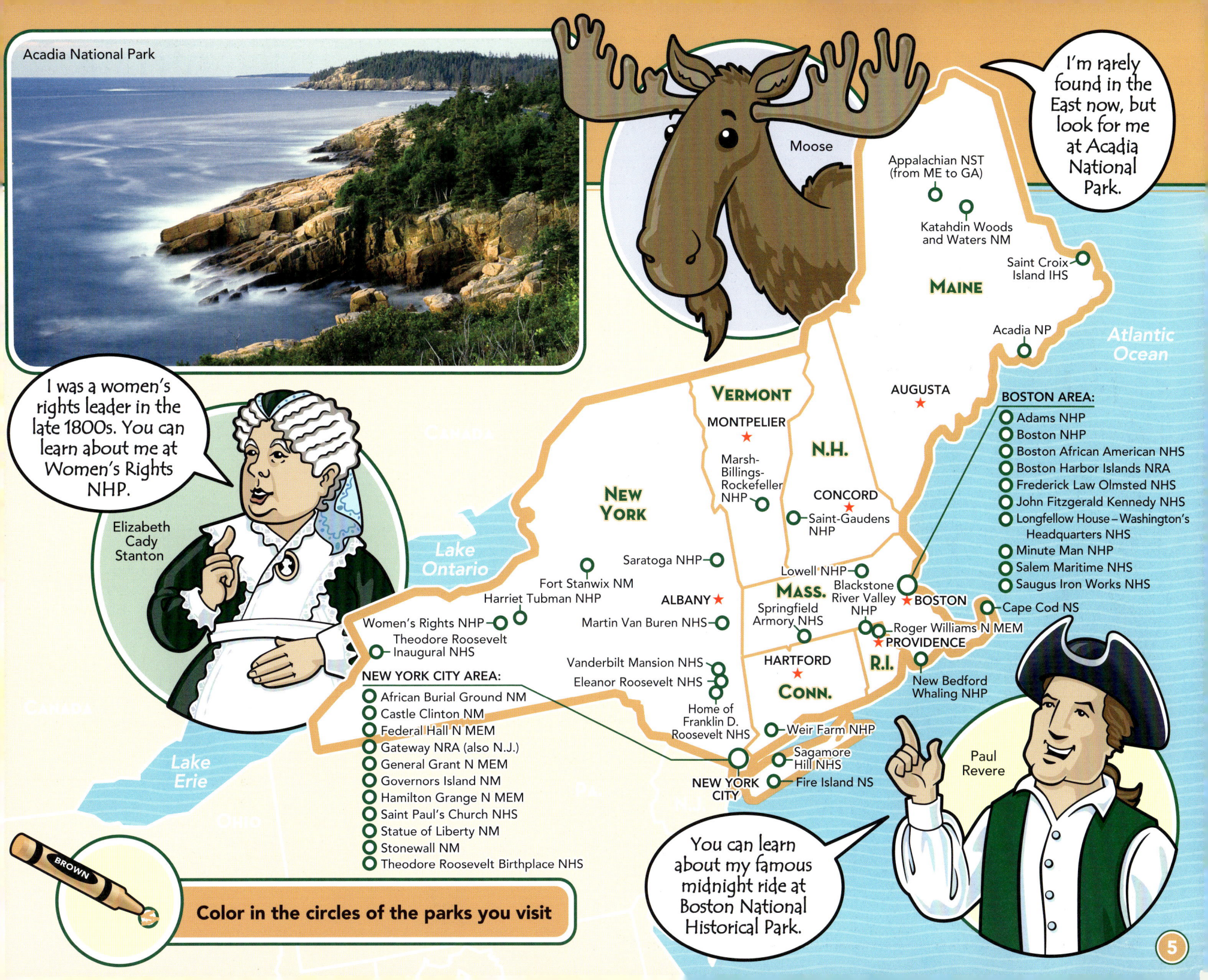

5

APPALACHIAN TRAIL

The **Appalachian Trail** begins—or ends—in Maine and goes through 14 states, all the way to Georgia. Some hardy "thru-hikers" walk the entire 2,175 miles from end to end, but there are lots of places to get on and off the trail for people who enjoy short hikes.

The Appalachian Trail is a national scenic trail because of the beautiful scenery you can see from high in the Appalachian Mountains along the way. There are other kinds of national trails, too. National historic trails, like the Star-Spangled Banner NHT commemorating the War of 1812, follow routes of historical importance. National recreation trails are places that offer lots of ways to have fun outdoors.

There are national trails in all 50 states. You can find one near you and learn about the National Trails System at nps.gov/nts

Nature Hunt

When you are out on a hike, whether on a national trail or just in your neighborhood, take a look around and see if you can find these animals, plants, or natural objects.

Make a check mark in the box next to the nature objects below. How many can you find?

- ☐ Squirrel
- ☐ Frog
- ☐ Turtle
- ☐ Log
- ☐ Acorn
- ☐ Oak Leaf
- ☐ Hawk or Eagle
- ☐ Fiddlehead Fern
- ☐ Dragonfly
- ☐ Butterfly
- ☐ Maple Leaf
- ☐ Pine Cone
- ☐ Seedpod
- ☐ Animal Paw Print
- ☐ Feather
- ☐ Bird
- ☐ Dandelion

THEME: Revolutionary War

America Rebels!

The American War for Independence changed the course of history. In the eight-year war, from 1775 to 1783, colonists wanting independence and a new democratic republic rebelled against Great Britain, which wanted to keep the colonies in its powerful empire.

The initial "shot heard 'round the world" was fired in Massachusetts, but it echoed through all the colonies and beyond.

Step into History

Today, you can visit many of the places where the Revolution happened. Walk along the 2.5-mile Freedom Trail in Boston NHP to see the Old North Church and other sites on the road to revolution. In Philadelphia, you can see the famous Liberty Bell and stand in the very room where the founding fathers signed the Declaration of Independence. At national park battlefields from Massachusetts to South Carolina you can learn how the ragtag colonists managed to defeat the mighty British.

Most of the action took place in the eastern states that were once British colonies. But many other places also have roots in the American Revolution. For example, George Rogers Clark NHP in Indiana tells how Americans captured a British fort and opened the way to westward expansion. Washington, DC, exists because victorious Americans made good on their promise to form a new kind of government.

You can learn all about the American Revolution and the parks to visit at nps.gov/subjects/americanrevolution/index.htm

Valley Forge National Historical Park

Minute Man National Historical Park

Independence National Historical Park

Mid-Atlantic Region

Liberty Bell Word•Find

- America
- Benjamin Franklin
- Constitution
- Eagle
- Fife and Drum
- Founding Fathers
- Freedom
- George Washington
- Government
- Independence
- John Adams
- Liberty Bell
- National Park
- Philadelphia
- Presidents
- Revolution
- Thomas Jefferson
- United States

National Parks in the Mid-Atlantic Region

So much of what you learn when you study American history happened right here in the Mid-Atlantic Region. Many of this region's national parks tell stories of the high points and low points of building a new nation.

Here you can visit Jamestown, site of the first permanent English settlement in America. See battlefields from four different wars: the French and Indian War, the American Revolution, the War of 1812, and the Civil War.

Here you will find cherished symbols of the United States—the Liberty Bell at Independence NHP and Fort McHenry, which inspired the "Star-Spangled Banner." You can visit the homes of famous Americans, such as Dwight D. Eisenhower, Booker T. Washington, and Edgar Allan Poe.

With so much history everywhere, it's easy to forget that the Mid-Atlantic Region also includes plenty of places to enjoy nature. Travel the scenic Skyline Drive through Shenandoah NP, take to the water at Delaware Water Gap NRA, or watch wild horses frolic at Assateague Island NS. These are just a few of the things to do in this region's varied parks.

Did You Know?

- The Liberty Bell was known as the State House Bell at the time that America declared its independence. It wasn't called the Liberty Bell until more than 60 years later when it became a symbol for ending enslavement in America.

- President Abraham Lincoln delivered the Gettysburg Address to dedicate a national cemetery for soldiers who died at the Battle of Gettysburg. Lincoln's speech lasted about two minutes and is one of the best-known speeches in American history.

- Clara Barton, founder of the American Red Cross, had no formal medical training, yet she set up field hospitals and tended to wounded soldiers during the Civil War. She later led relief efforts after floods, fires, and other disasters in this country and abroad. Learn more at Clara Barton NHS in Maryland and Johnstown Flood N MEM in Pennsylvania.

- Families lived on board their boats when they worked the Chesapeake and Ohio Canal. Entire families stayed in a room about 12 feet square. A smaller area provided shelter for the mules. Take a boat ride on the historic C&O Canal and imagine growing up in a canal family.

I'm famous for writing scary stories.

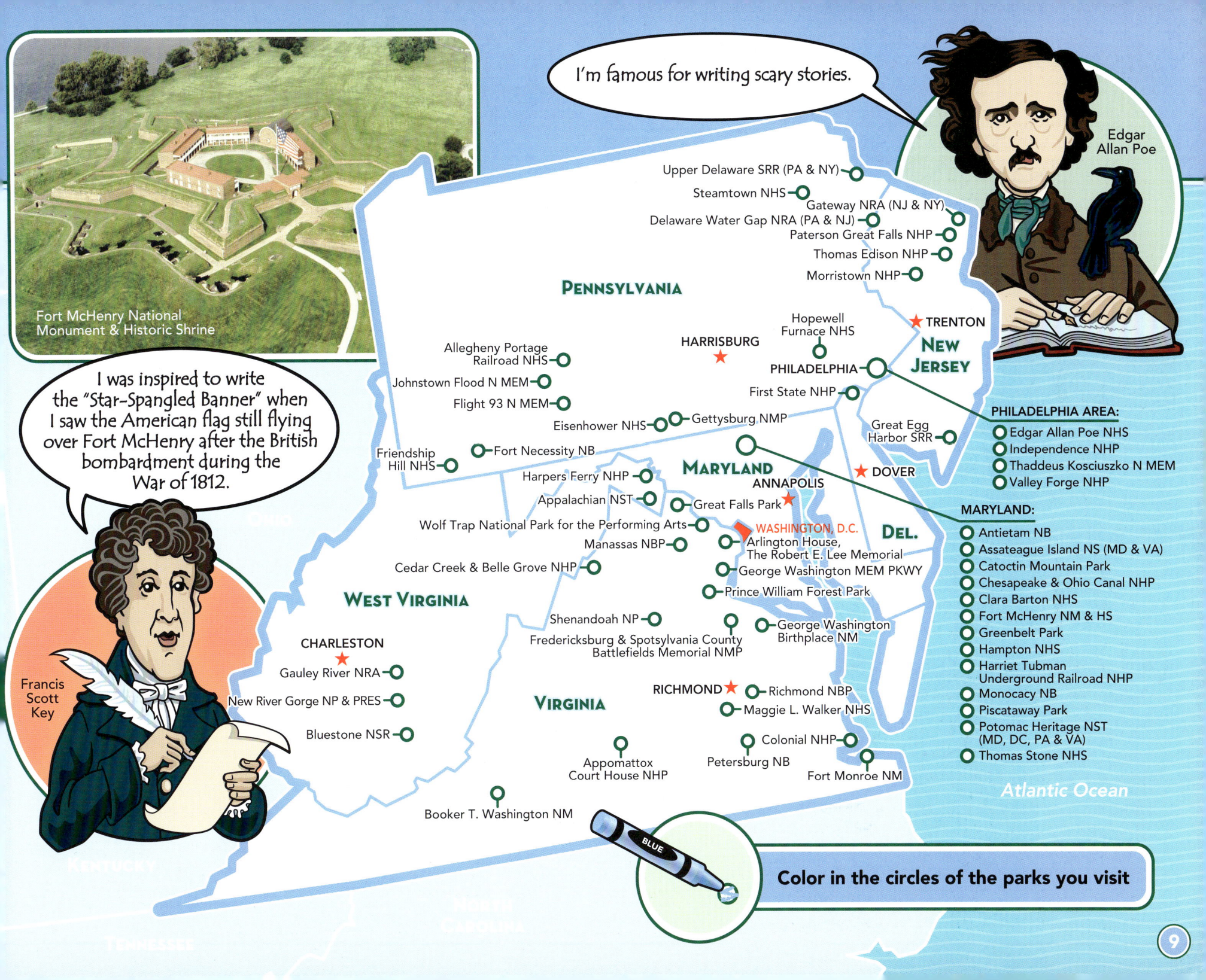

Edgar Allan Poe

Fort McHenry National Monument & Historic Shrine

I was inspired to write the "Star-Spangled Banner" when I saw the American flag still flying over Fort McHenry after the British bombardment during the War of 1812.

Francis Scott Key

PENNSYLVANIA

- Upper Delaware SRR (PA & NY)
- Steamtown NHS
- Gateway NRA (NJ & NY)
- Delaware Water Gap NRA (PA & NJ)
- Paterson Great Falls NHP
- Thomas Edison NHP
- Morristown NHP
- Hopewell Furnace NHS
- Allegheny Portage Railroad NHS
- Johnstown Flood N MEM
- Flight 93 N MEM
- Eisenhower NHS
- Gettysburg NMP
- First State NHP
- Great Egg Harbor SRR
- Friendship Hill NHS
- Fort Necessity NB

★ HARRISBURG
★ PHILADELPHIA
★ TRENTON

NEW JERSEY

MARYLAND
- Harpers Ferry NHP
- Appalachian NST
- Great Falls Park
- Wolf Trap National Park for the Performing Arts
- Manassas NBP
- Cedar Creek & Belle Grove NHP

★ ANNAPOLIS
★ DOVER
WASHINGTON, D.C.
- Arlington House, The Robert E. Lee Memorial
- George Washington MEM PKWY
- Prince William Forest Park

DEL.

WEST VIRGINIA
- Shenandoah NP
- Fredericksburg & Spotsylvania County Battlefields Memorial NMP
- George Washington Birthplace NM

★ CHARLESTON
- Gauley River NRA
- New River Gorge NP & PRES
- Bluestone NSR

★ RICHMOND
- Richmond NBP
- Maggie L. Walker NHS

VIRGINIA
- Colonial NHP
- Petersburg NB
- Appomattox Court House NHP
- Fort Monroe NM
- Booker T. Washington NM

PHILADELPHIA AREA:
- Edgar Allan Poe NHS
- Independence NHP
- Thaddeus Kosciuszko N MEM
- Valley Forge NHP

MARYLAND:
- Antietam NB
- Assateague Island NS (MD & VA)
- Catoctin Mountain Park
- Chesapeake & Ohio Canal NHP
- Clara Barton NHS
- Fort McHenry NM & HS
- Greenbelt Park
- Hampton NHS
- Harriet Tubman Underground Railroad NHP
- Monocacy NB
- Piscataway Park
- Potomac Heritage NST (MD, DC, PA & VA)
- Thomas Stone NHS

Atlantic Ocean

BLUE

Color in the circles of the parks you visit

9

Transportation and Industry in America

Even before the Revolutionary War ended, a different kind of revolution started in Europe and America. The steam engine and other inventions brought the Industrial Revolution, which continued through most of the 19th century.

Invention of the cotton gin meant the South could produce more cotton for northern markets. Textile mills opened in New England. The sewing machine led to factory-made clothing. The use of standard parts and assembly lines improved efficiency in all types of manufacturing. Busy factories needed more workers. Cities grew rapidly as people came from rural America and other countries.

Industry needed better transportation. Young America was on the move, building roads, railroads, and water routes to open the way to new markets and supplies.

Many national parks tell how industry and transportation changed America. In this region, visit the laboratories of inventor Thomas Edison. Learn about iron making at Hopewell Furnace NHS. Visit C&O Canal NHP, Steamtown NHS, and Allegheny Portage Railroad NHS to discover why railroads beat the canals in a race to the west.

In other regions, don't miss Lowell NHP to learn about young workers in the mills. Visit Ellis Island to learn about immigrants who came to work in America. In Michigan, visit Keweenaw NHP to see what industrial mining was like in the 1800s and 1900s. At Golden Spike NHP in Utah, learn about the first railroads to cross America.

Lowell National Historical Park

All Aboard!

Learn all about America's early railroads at Steamtown and Allegheny Portage Railroad national historic sites in Pennsylvania. You might even get to ride a train! Color the steam train pictured below.

Steamtown National Historic Site

THEME: CIVIL WAR

THE NORTH

General Ulysses S. Grant

THE WAR BETWEEN THE STATES

The first military action of the Civil War took place at Fort Sumter, in Charleston, SC, on April 12, 1861.

For four tragic years, the nation was torn apart in a bitter civil war. The North and South had different ideas about government and the issue of slavery. In April 1861, southern states broke away to attempt to form a separate country. The North fought to preserve the Union, and later to end enslavement.

Although the devastating war affected everyone, it was especially hard for the middle states, which were major battlegrounds. Union and Confederate capitals and vital supply lines were located here. Border states were truly dividing lines, often with brother fighting brother and father fighting son. In Virginia, the differences were so great that western counties formed a new state, West Virginia.

More than 70 national park sites help tell the stories of the American Civil War. Many are in the Mid-Atlantic Region, but you can learn about the Civil War in other areas as well—from Fort Sumter and Fort Moultrie NHP in the East to Fort Point NHS in the West. There is no better way to understand the American Civil War than to visit the real places where it happened.

For Civil War parks and events, visit the National Park Service website: nps.gov/civilwar

THE SOUTH

General Robert E. Lee

Confederate General Robert E. Lee surrendered to General Ulysses S. Grant at Appomattox Court House, VA, on April 9, 1865.

National Capital Region

Find the Differences

These two drawings look the same, but they're not! Can you find 12 differences between the top and bottom drawings?

National Parks in the National Capital Region

Nowhere else in America will you find so many monuments and historic places as in the Nation's Capital. Washington, DC, was designed to hold America's treasures.

George Washington chose the location and asked Pierre L'Enfant to design a capital city for the new nation. At Freedom Plaza, you can stand on a large map of L'Enfant's plan. Look for the National Mall at the city's center, with the Capitol at one end. Follow Pennsylvania Avenue from there to the White House. Diagonal streets create little parks at their centers. If you go to the top of the Old Post Office Tower or the Washington Monument and look down, you'll see how closely the city follows the original plan.

People come to Washington to honor the past and see places where history is still made. While you are here, take time to discover Rock Creek Park, one of the nation's oldest and largest city parks.

It's easy to get around in Washington. You can walk or take a fast trip on the underground Metro.

Did You Know?

- A free African American, Benjamin Banneker, helped to survey land for the new capital city. He was an inventor and publisher, too.

- British troops invaded Washington during the War of 1812 and burned the White House and other important buildings.

- The walls at the base of the Washington Monument are 15 feet thick. The monument was the tallest masonry structure in the world when it was completed in 1884.

- Franklin Delano Roosevelt was diagnosed with polio at age 39. He used a wheelchair for all of his 12 years as president. You can see a life-size statue of Roosevelt at the FDR Memorial.

- During World War I, gardeners were hard to find. President Wilson let sheep graze the White House grounds to trim the grass. Money from the sale of the sheep's wool was given to the Red Cross for soldiers' uniforms.

- Memorial Bridge, which crosses the Potomac River, was built as a symbol of the reunited Union after the Civil War. It connects the Lincoln Memorial to Arlington House, the home of Confederate General Robert E. Lee.

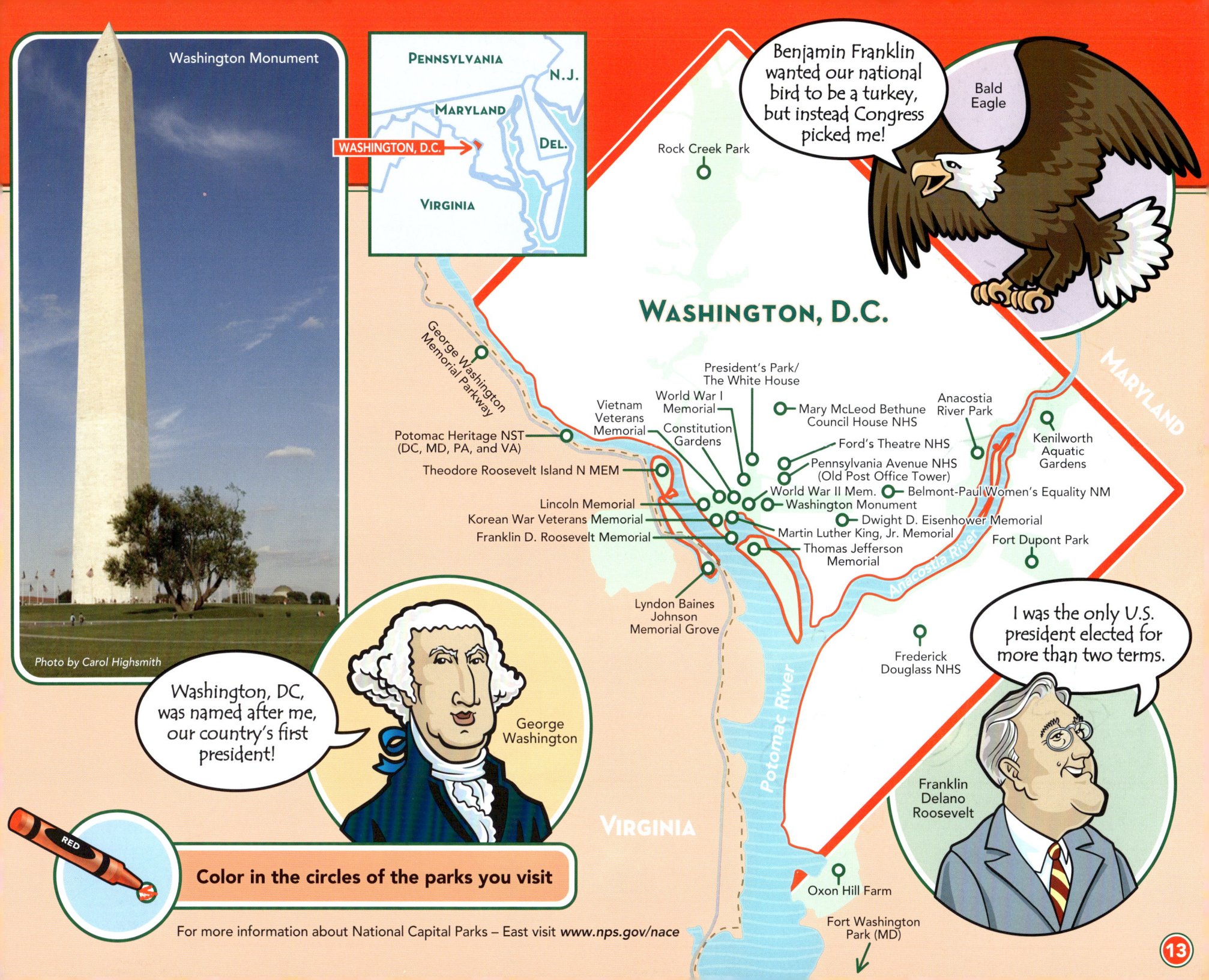

Washington, D.C.

Washington Monument
Photo by Carol Highsmith

Benjamin Franklin wanted our national bird to be a turkey, but instead Congress picked me! — Bald Eagle

Washington, DC, was named after me, our country's first president! — George Washington

I was the only U.S. president elected for more than two terms. — Franklin Delano Roosevelt

Locations shown on map:
- Rock Creek Park
- George Washington Memorial Parkway
- Potomac Heritage NST (DC, MD, PA, and VA)
- Theodore Roosevelt Island N MEM
- Vietnam Veterans Memorial
- World War I Memorial
- Constitution Gardens
- President's Park/The White House
- Mary McLeod Bethune Council House NHS
- Anacostia River Park
- Ford's Theatre NHS
- Pennsylvania Avenue NHS (Old Post Office Tower)
- Kenilworth Aquatic Gardens
- Lincoln Memorial
- World War II Mem.
- Belmont-Paul Women's Equality NM
- Korean War Veterans Memorial
- Washington Monument
- Dwight D. Eisenhower Memorial
- Franklin D. Roosevelt Memorial
- Martin Luther King, Jr. Memorial
- Fort Dupont Park
- Thomas Jefferson Memorial
- Lyndon Baines Johnson Memorial Grove
- Frederick Douglass NHS
- Oxon Hill Farm
- Fort Washington Park (MD)

Color in the circles of the parks you visit

For more information about National Capital Parks – East visit www.nps.gov/nace

The Right to Vote

Washington, DC, is full of symbols of America's government. That's why the city is often the place where people gather to draw attention to their causes. The National Mall, the Capitol and White House, even the steps of the Lincoln Memorial have been the stage for marches and rallies as people come together to express their opinions.

In the early 1900s, many people came to Washington seeking to change the U.S. Constitution to allow women the right to vote. Originally, only white men could vote. An amendment to the Constitution in 1870 gave the vote to black men, but it took 50 years more before the 19th amendment let women vote. During that time, there were many demonstrations in Washington. In 1916, a group of women even chained themselves to the White House fence in protest.

Women's Rights NHP, which is dedicated to telling this important story, is located in New York. But while you are in Washington, you can visit several places to learn about women's struggles for equality. Belmont-Paul Women's Equality NM offers programs for young people at its museum. At the Mary McLeod Bethune Council House you can learn about a leader in black women's rights. At Frederick Douglass NHS, you'll hear how this former slave fought for women's rights as well as the rights of African Americans. And at the Franklin Delano Roosevelt Memorial, you can learn about First Lady Eleanor Roosevelt, a strong supporter of equal rights.

Because of the struggles of many people, today any American citizen who is at least 18 years old has the right to vote in national elections. It is the greatest privilege—and responsibility—of being a U.S. citizen.

Mary McLeod Bethune

Eleanor Roosevelt

Climb the Steps of the Lincoln Memorial

Can you answer these trivia questions as you climb the steps of the Lincoln Memorial?

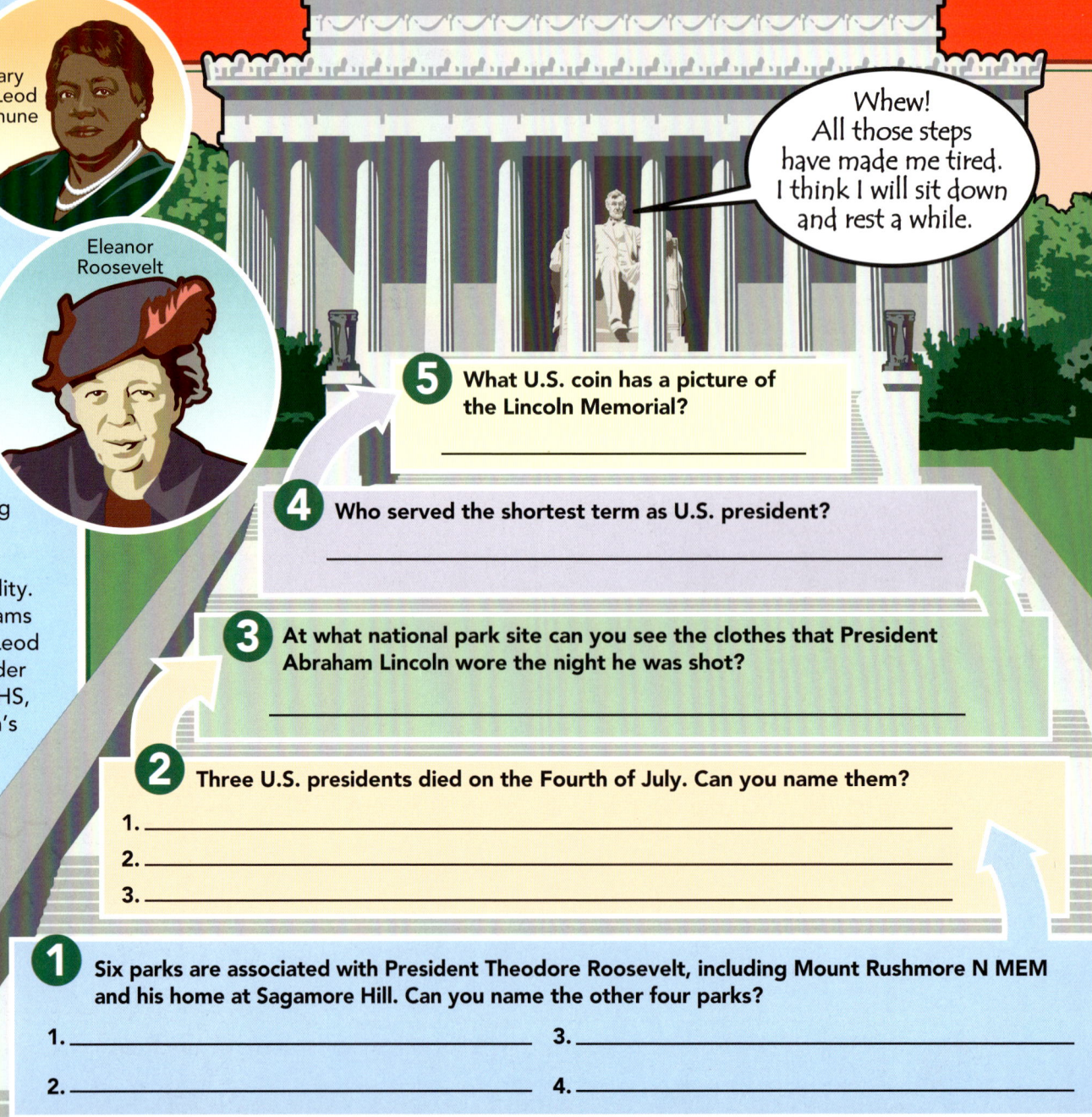

Whew! All those steps have made me tired. I think I will sit down and rest a while.

5 What U.S. coin has a picture of the Lincoln Memorial?
_____

4 Who served the shortest term as U.S. president?
_____

3 At what national park site can you see the clothes that President Abraham Lincoln wore the night he was shot?
_____

2 Three U.S. presidents died on the Fourth of July. Can you name them?
1. _____
2. _____
3. _____

1 Six parks are associated with President Theodore Roosevelt, including Mount Rushmore N MEM and his home at Sagamore Hill. Can you name the other four parks?
1. _____   3. _____
2. _____   4. _____

THEME: PRESIDENTS

Draw a fifth face on the monument. Who would you add? Perhaps you will be president one day!

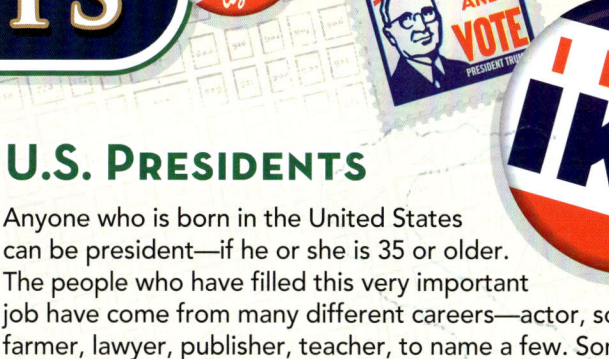

U.S. Presidents

Anyone who is born in the United States can be president—if he or she is 35 or older. The people who have filled this very important job have come from many different careers—actor, soldier, farmer, lawyer, publisher, teacher, to name a few. Some came from wealthy families, but most grew up in ordinary homes. It is fun to visit the birthplaces and childhood homes of presidents to learn how their backgrounds helped shape their future presidency.

Nearly every region of the country has places you can visit to learn more about America's presidents. Look at the regional lists of national park sites in this book to see how many you can find.

Every president except one—George Washington—has lived in the President's House in Washington, DC. We now call it the White House, and it is very grand compared to the presidents' own homes. Can you imagine living in a house with 132 rooms, 35 bathrooms, 3 kitchens, 28 fireplaces, a medical clinic and dental office, a swimming pool, a tennis court, a movie theater, and a bowling alley?

Mount Rushmore

Mount Rushmore National Memorial is located in Keystone, South Dakota. It was carved into a mountain by a man named Gutzon Borglum, and was completed in 1941.

Can you name the four presidents who appear on Mount Rushmore?

1. _____
2. _____
3. _____
4. _____

The White House is located in a national park—President's Park—and it is on one of the most famous streets in the world: historic Pennsylvania Avenue.

SOUTHEAST REGION

CONNECT the DOTS

Connect the dots to find out which creature lives in Everglades National Park in Florida.

START HERE

Color in the picture, and add a background. What other creatures live in the Everglades?

NATIONAL PARKS IN THE SOUTHEAST REGION

The Southeast Region has more national parks than any other region. You can learn so many different stories here. There are places where battles in the American Revolution were fought—such as Kings Mountain NMP and Moores Creek NB. There are also places where battles in the Civil War were fought, such as where the war began at Fort Sumter and the site of the bloody battle of Shiloh.

You can see forts and other sites where different countries tried to claim ownership of America—the English in Georgia and the Carolinas, the Spanish and French in Florida, the Danes in the Caribbean. You can visit places that tell about the struggles of African Americans for freedom and equal rights.

This region also has some of the nation's most beautiful beaches and underwater sites. You can see rare and colorful birds and other unusual wildlife in the Everglades and at Big Cypress National Preserve.

From the heights of Great Smoky Mountains NP to the depths of Mammoth Cave NP, you'll never run out of new things to discover in the parks of the Southeast Region.

DID YOU KNOW?

- Everglades NP is the only place in the world where alligators and crocodiles live side by side.

- Mammoth Cave NP in Kentucky is the longest known cave system in the world. More than 365 miles have been mapped underground.

- At Wright Brothers N MEM in North Carolina, you can learn why Wilbur and Orville Wright chose Kitty Hawk for their experiments with airplanes. The same winds and sand make this a popular place for kite flying and hang gliding today.

- The giant hardwood trees in Congaree NP in South Carolina are some of the oldest and tallest in the world. Before people cut down forests for lumber and farms, nearly all of the eastern United States would have looked like this.

- In the early 1800s, boatmen called "Kaintucks" floated livestock and coal down the Ohio and Mississippi rivers on flatboats. At Natchez or New Orleans they took the boats apart to sell the wood; then they walked some 500 miles back north. You can follow their route along the scenic Natchez Trace Parkway.

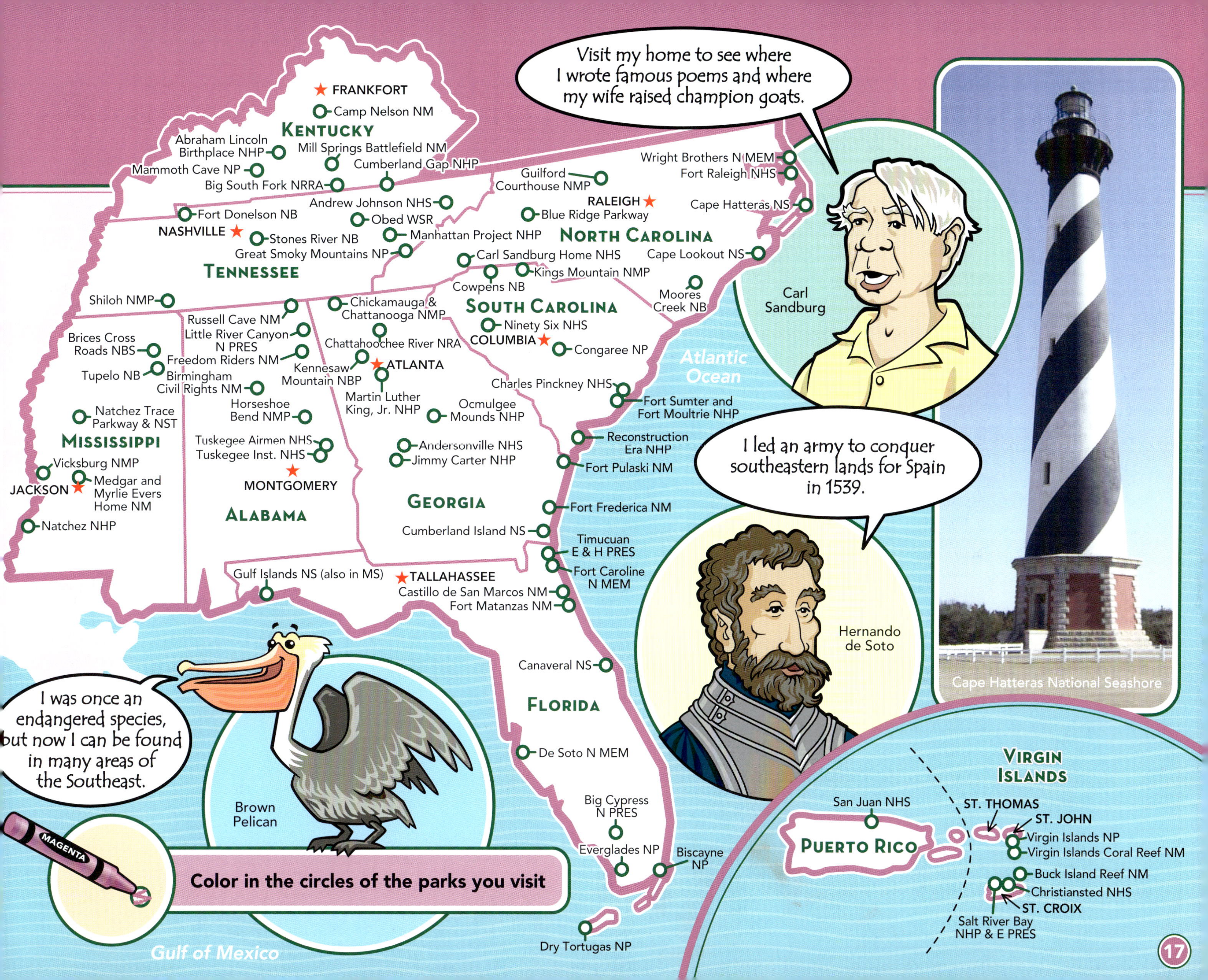

Visit my home to see where I wrote famous poems and where my wife raised champion goats.
Carl Sandburg
I led an army to conquer southeastern lands for Spain in 1539.
Hernando de Soto
I was once an endangered species, but now I can be found in many areas of the Southeast.
Brown Pelican
MAGENTA
Color in the circles of the parks you visit
Cape Hatteras National Seashore
KENTUCKY
FRANKFORT
Camp Nelson NM
Abraham Lincoln Birthplace NHP
Mill Springs Battlefield NM
Mammoth Cave NP
Cumberland Gap NHP
Big South Fork NRRA
TENNESSEE
Fort Donelson NB
NASHVILLE
Stones River NB
Andrew Johnson NHS
Obed WSR
Manhattan Project NHP
Great Smoky Mountains NP
Shiloh NMP
NORTH CAROLINA
Wright Brothers N MEM
Fort Raleigh NHS
Guilford Courthouse NMP
RALEIGH
Blue Ridge Parkway
Cape Hatteras NS
Cape Lookout NS
Carl Sandburg Home NHS
Kings Mountain NMP
Moores Creek NB
SOUTH CAROLINA
Cowpens NB
Ninety Six NHS
COLUMBIA
Congaree NP
Charles Pinckney NHS
Fort Sumter and Fort Moultrie NHP
Reconstruction Era NHP
Atlantic Ocean
MISSISSIPPI
Brices Cross Roads NBS
Tupelo NB
Natchez Trace Parkway & NST
Vicksburg NMP
JACKSON
Medgar and Myrlie Evers Home NM
Natchez NHP
ALABAMA
Russell Cave NM
Little River Canyon N PRES
Freedom Riders NM
Birmingham Civil Rights NM
Horseshoe Bend NMP
Tuskegee Airmen NHS
Tuskegee Inst. NHS
MONTGOMERY
GEORGIA
Chickamauga & Chattanooga NMP
Chattahoochee River NRA
Kennesaw Mountain NBP
ATLANTA
Martin Luther King, Jr. NHP
Ocmulgee Mounds NHP
Andersonville NHS
Jimmy Carter NHP
Fort Pulaski NM
Fort Frederica NM
Cumberland Island NS
FLORIDA
Timucuan E & H PRES
Fort Caroline N MEM
Gulf Islands NS (also in MS)
TALLAHASSEE
Castillo de San Marcos NM
Fort Matanzas NM
Canaveral NS
De Soto N MEM
Big Cypress N PRES
Everglades NP
Biscayne NP
Dry Tortugas NP
Gulf of Mexico
PUERTO RICO
San Juan NHS
VIRGIN ISLANDS
ST. THOMAS
ST. JOHN
Virgin Islands NP
Virgin Islands Coral Reef NM
Buck Island Reef NM
Christiansted NHS
ST. CROIX
Salt River Bay NHP & E PRES

Forts in the National Parks

There are more than 25 forts in the National Park System where you can learn about different periods of history.

In the forts along the southeastern coast, for example, you can learn how the Spanish tried to protect St. Augustine, the first permanent European settlement in North America. Fort Caroline tells how the French tried to make a foothold in Florida; Fort Frederica represents the English and Spanish rivalry for coastal territory.

Stories of conflicts in the English colonies are told at Fort Necessity and Fort Stanwix. Fort McHenry protected Baltimore from the British in the War of 1812. Civil War forts, such as Fort Pulaski and Fort Donelson, protected supply routes and important cities. Across the country in California, Fort Point was a Civil War-period fort that also served in World War II.

Many forts were built during the nation's movement westward in the 19th century to protect frontier borders for settlers, travelers, and trade. Places like Fort Scott and Fort Laramie tell about the harsh realities of life in the West.

You can learn a lot about the early settlement and growth of this country by visiting historic forts.

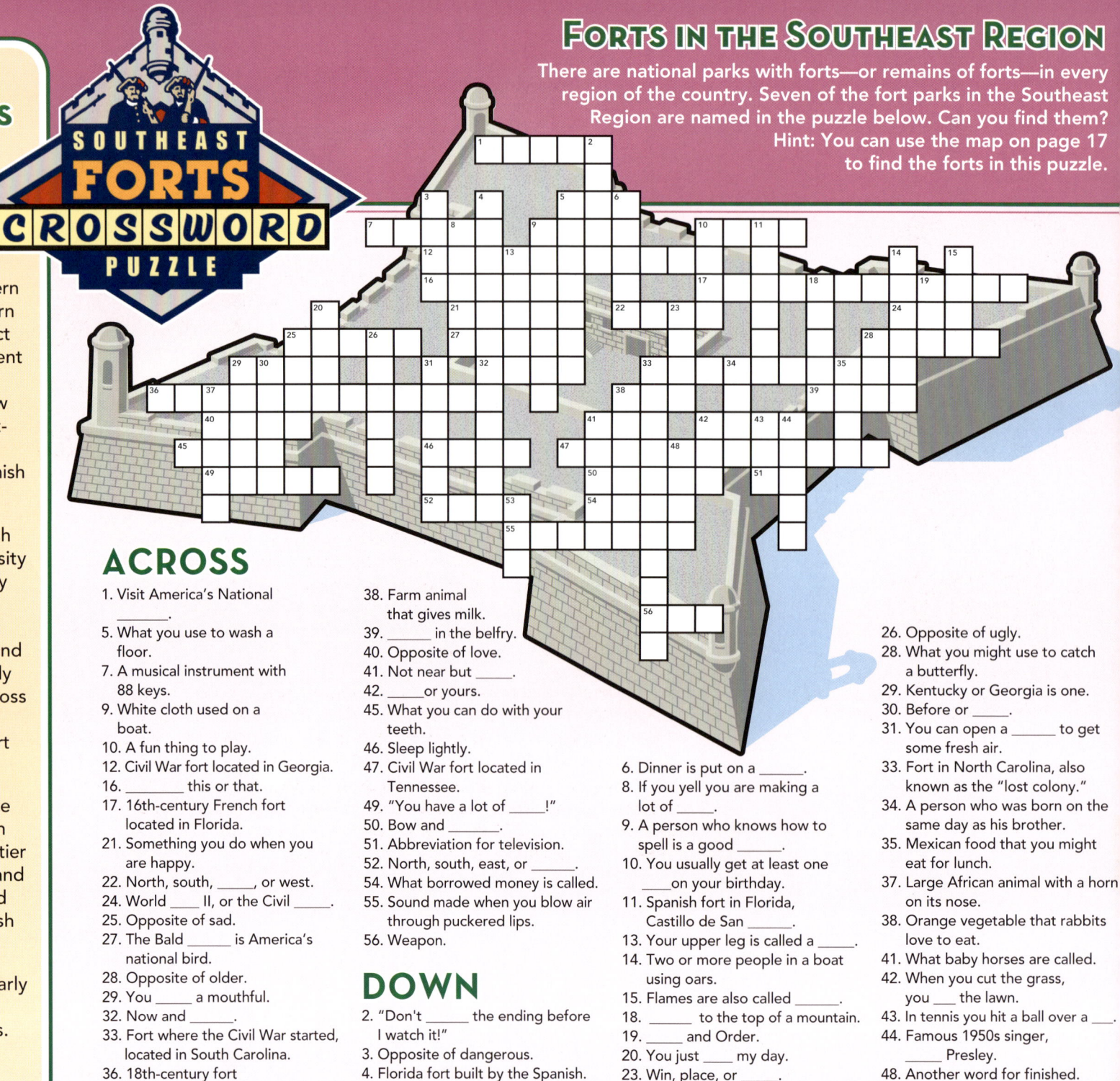

Southeast Forts Crossword Puzzle

Forts in the Southeast Region

There are national parks with forts—or remains of forts—in every region of the country. Seven of the fort parks in the Southeast Region are named in the puzzle below. Can you find them?
Hint: You can use the map on page 17 to find the forts in this puzzle.

ACROSS

1. Visit America's National _____.
5. What you use to wash a floor.
7. A musical instrument with 88 keys.
9. White cloth used on a boat.
10. A fun thing to play.
12. Civil War fort located in Georgia.
16. _____ this or that.
17. 16th-century French fort located in Florida.
21. Something you do when you are happy.
22. North, south, _____, or west.
24. World _____ II, or the Civil _____.
25. Opposite of sad.
27. The Bald _____ is America's national bird.
28. Opposite of older.
29. You _____ a mouthful.
32. Now and _____.
33. Fort where the Civil War started, located in South Carolina.
36. 18th-century fort located in Georgia.
38. Farm animal that gives milk.
39. _____ in the belfry.
40. Opposite of love.
41. Not near but _____.
42. _____ or yours.
45. What you can do with your teeth.
46. Sleep lightly.
47. Civil War fort located in Tennessee.
49. "You have a lot of _____!"
50. Bow and _____.
51. Abbreviation for television.
52. North, south, east, or _____.
54. What borrowed money is called.
55. Sound made when you blow air through puckered lips.
56. Weapon.

DOWN

2. "Don't _____ the ending before I watch it!"
3. Opposite of dangerous.
4. Florida fort built by the Spanish.
5. Irish girl's name.
6. Dinner is put on a _____.
8. If you yell you are making a lot of _____.
9. A person who knows how to spell is a good _____.
10. You usually get at least one _____ on your birthday.
11. Spanish fort in Florida, Castillo de San _____.
13. Your upper leg is called a _____.
14. Two or more people in a boat using oars.
15. Flames are also called _____.
18. _____ to the top of a mountain.
19. _____ and Order.
20. You just _____ my day.
23. Win, place, or _____.
25. A boss might _____ you for a job.
26. Opposite of ugly.
28. What you might use to catch a butterfly.
29. Kentucky or Georgia is one.
30. Before or _____.
31. You can open a _____ to get some fresh air.
33. Fort in North Carolina, also known as the "lost colony."
34. A person who was born on the same day as his brother.
35. Mexican food that you might eat for lunch.
37. Large African animal with a horn on its nose.
38. Orange vegetable that rabbits love to eat.
41. What baby horses are called.
42. When you cut the grass, you _____ the lawn.
43. In tennis you hit a ball over a _____.
44. Famous 1950s singer, _____ Presley.
48. Another word for finished.
53. One, _____, three.

18

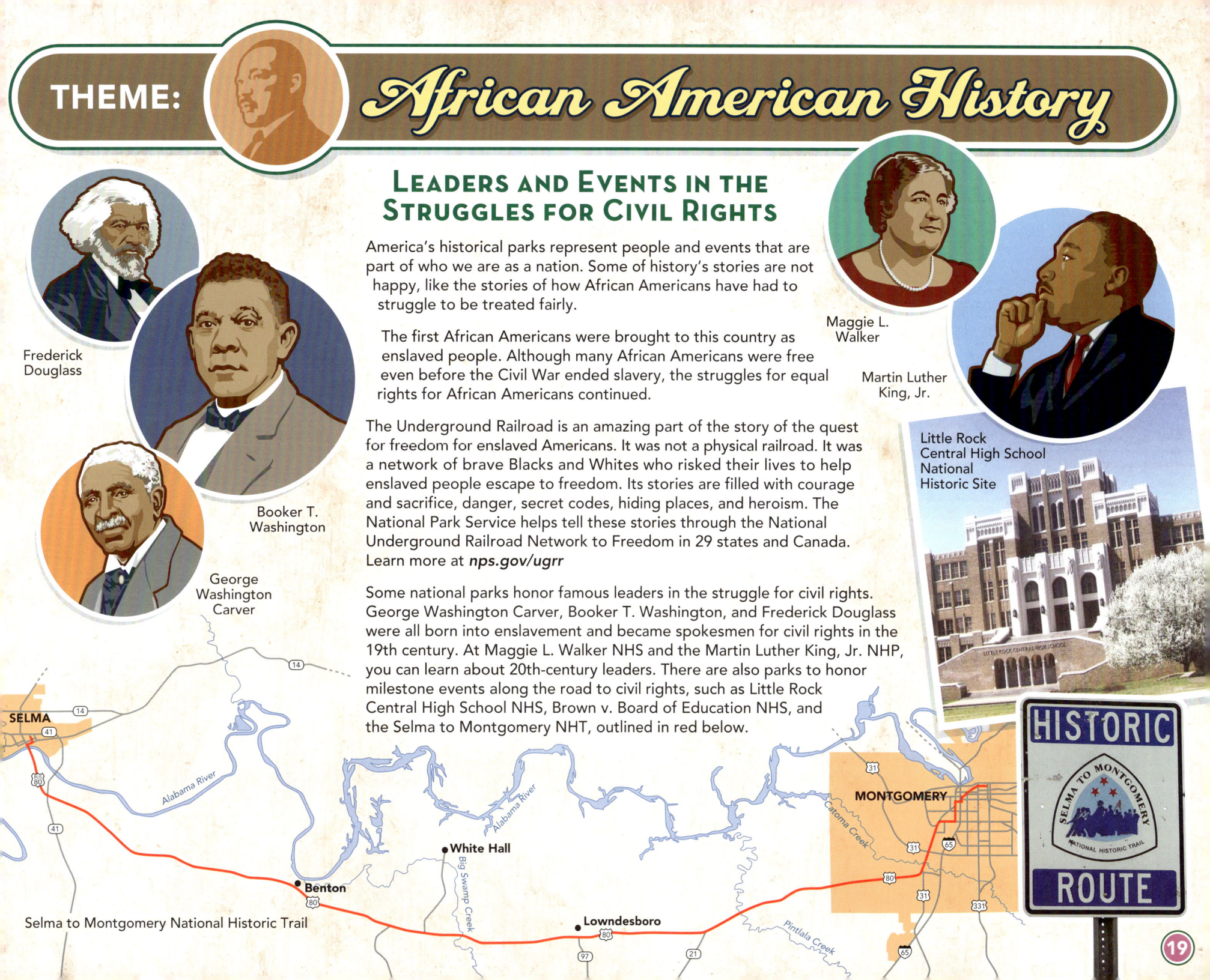

THEME: African American History

Leaders and Events in the Struggles for Civil Rights

America's historical parks represent people and events that are part of who we are as a nation. Some of history's stories are not happy, like the stories of how African Americans have had to struggle to be treated fairly.

The first African Americans were brought to this country as enslaved people. Although many African Americans were free even before the Civil War ended slavery, the struggles for equal rights for African Americans continued.

The Underground Railroad is an amazing part of the story of the quest for freedom for enslaved Americans. It was not a physical railroad. It was a network of brave Blacks and Whites who risked their lives to help enslaved people escape to freedom. Its stories are filled with courage and sacrifice, danger, secret codes, hiding places, and heroism. The National Park Service helps tell these stories through the National Underground Railroad Network to Freedom in 29 states and Canada. Learn more at *nps.gov/ugrr*

Some national parks honor famous leaders in the struggle for civil rights. George Washington Carver, Booker T. Washington, and Frederick Douglass were all born into enslavement and became spokesmen for civil rights in the 19th century. At Maggie L. Walker NHS and the Martin Luther King, Jr. NHP, you can learn about 20th-century leaders. There are also parks to honor milestone events along the road to civil rights, such as Little Rock Central High School NHS, Brown v. Board of Education NHS, and the Selma to Montgomery NHT, outlined in red below.

Frederick Douglass

Booker T. Washington

George Washington Carver

Maggie L. Walker

Martin Luther King, Jr.

Little Rock Central High School National Historic Site

Selma to Montgomery National Historic Trail

HISTORIC ROUTE

Midwest Region

First Ladies Match Game

- Mary Todd
- Lady Bird
- Martha
- Dolley
- Jacqueline

- George Washington — President from 1789-1797
- James Madison — President from 1809-1817
- Abraham Lincoln — President from 1861-1865
- John Fitzgerald Kennedy — President from 1961-1963
- Lyndon Baines Johnson — President from 1963-1969

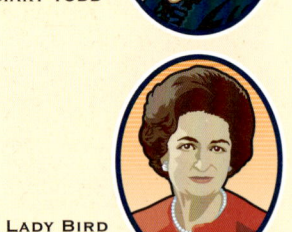

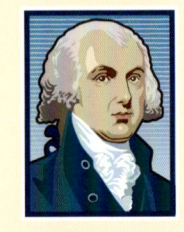

Draw a line to match each first lady with her husband, the president. Many first ladies have had important roles in addition to being hostess at the White House. Visit First Ladies NHS in Canton, Ohio, to learn more.

National Parks in the Midwest Region

America's heartland holds a surprising variety of national parks. Often overshadowed by bigger parks in the eastern and western states, the Midwest Region offers superb natural, historical, and recreational sites that should not be missed.

Here you can learn about ancient mammals and early human cultures at Agate Fossil Beds NM, Hopewell Culture NHP, Effigy Mounds NM, and Pipestone NM. Visit Fort Larned NHS and learn how cultures clashed as the American frontier moved westward.

The Midwest has important battle sites from the American Revolution (George Rogers Clark NHP), from the War of 1812 (Perry's Victory and International Peace Memorial), and from the American Civil War (Wilson's Creek NB). There are seven homes of U.S. presidents in this region, plus a national historic site where you can learn about first ladies.

History follows along the region's rivers and lakes, which have always been important routes for commerce and travel. Cuyahoga Valley NP, national lakeshores, and national rivers such as the Mississippi, Ozark, and Niobrara offer great recreation and scenic beauty.

Take time to discover the variety in the Midwest's national parks.

Did You Know?

- Ancient Native Americans buried their dead in great mounds that were often built in the shapes of animals or birds. You can see many examples at Effigy Mounds NM in Iowa.

- The reddish stone found at Pipestone NM was used by members of Plains Tribes to carve ceremonial pipes. The quarries where the rock is found were sacred lands, and even enemy tribes would not fight there.

- First Lady Lucy Hayes was nicknamed "Lemonade Lucy." She and her husband, President Rutherford B. Hayes, banned alcoholic beverages at all White House functions.

- Dayton Aviation Heritage NHP honors three great Americans. Two of them—Wilbur and Orville Wright—are famous for inventing the first successful airplane. The third is Paul Laurence Dunbar, an important African American poet.

- The column of Perry's Victory and International Peace Memorial at Put-in-Bay, Ohio, is 47 feet taller than the Statue of Liberty.

- George Washington Carver was a former slave who later became an inventor. He found nearly 300 uses for peanuts.

Sleeping Bear Dunes National Lakeshore

1. ____________________
2. ____________________
3. ____________________
4. ____________________

Color in the circles of the parks you visit

Can you help the voyageur find his cabin, using only the waterways? Watch out for wild animals and beaver dams. If they block your path, you have to find another way.

Voyageurs Waterways

Exploring the Land of Opportunity

To people living in crowded cities of Europe, the North American continent was a new world of great abundance and adventure. Word traveled fast as explorers of various nationalities brought back tales of what they had seen here. De Soto's arrival in what is now Florida in 1539 and Cabrillo's expedition to what is now California in 1542 established claims for Spain. The English claimed the Mid-Atlantic coast with settlements at Fort Raleigh and at Jamestown. France established a settlement at Saint Croix Island in 1604 in what is now Maine and began to follow the northern waterways to explore what is now the border between Canada and the United States.

The Great Lakes were natural highways, which connected with river systems to carry explorers and settlers into the interior lands. The French and English used the Ohio, Missouri, Mississippi, and other rivers for travel and trade, just as the native people had done for centuries.

Many national parks preserve places important to the exploration and settlement of this nation. At parks in the Great Lakes region of the Midwest, you can get a feel for the wild, beautiful land the French explorers encountered and learn how they interacted with the native people. Places like Grand Portage NM, Voyageurs NP, Isle Royale NP, and the national lakeshore parks await your exploration and adventures as you imagine seeing this land as an explorer might have seen it for the first time.

THEME: Famous Americans

Can you match the famous person's head with the famous person's body?

- **A** Augustus Saint-Gaudens
- **B** Clara Barton
- **C** Thomas Alva Edison
- **D** Juan Rodriguez Cabrillo
- **E** Eleanor Roosevelt
- **F** Oliver Hazard Perry
- **G** Henry Wadsworth Longfellow

Artists, Writers, Inventors, Leaders, and Explorers

Many parks honor famous Americans who have made contributions important to the nation and the world. You'll find some in every region of the country. There are monuments, historic homes, and other national parks where you can learn about great writers, like Eugene O'Neill and Edgar Allan Poe; or artists like Thomas Cole, or the landscape architect Frederick Law Olmsted. Learn about Thomas A. Edison, the Wright Brothers, and other ingenious inventors at the very places where they made history. Other sites tell about men and women who stand out for their leadership in politics, war, human rights, or exploration.

Look at the parks on each of the maps in this book and see how many are named for individual people. Now look up their names on the National Park Service website at *www.nps.gov* to learn what the person did to earn a park in his or her name.

- **EXPLORER** from Spain who arrived in California in 1542
- **INVENTOR** who invented the light bulb and phonograph
- **FIRST LADY** from 1933–1945 who fought for civil rights and human rights
- **COMMODORE** (Navy Commander) during the War of 1812
- **CIVIL WAR NURSE** who founded the American Red Cross
- **POET** who wrote "Paul Revere's Ride" and "Evangeline"
- **ARTIST** who sculpted many Civil War monuments

Southwest Region

PETROGLYPHS

Petroglyphs are ancient carvings on rock walls. Some are recognizable as animals or people; others are complex symbols whose meaning remains a mystery. What do you think these petroglyphs mean?

DRAW YOUR OWN PETROGLYPHS:

National Parks in the Southwest Region

The Southwest is a region of contrasts of landscapes and cultures. In the eastern part you'll find lush green lands fed by the Mississippi River. Sample the beauty of this area at Hot Springs NP where you can hike the trails and then refresh in historic mineral baths. Travel west and discover different types of landscapes. The sandy beaches along the Gulf Coast, rock formations at El Malpais NM, the underground maze at Carlsbad Caverns, Guadalupe Mountains rising out of the desert, and gleaming dunes at White Sands NM are examples of this region's diverse natural areas.

This is a region of great cultural diversity, too. Historic sites tell of the mingling or clashing of cultures. For example, San Antonio Missions NHP represents Spanish attempts to colonize the Southwest. Palo Alto Battlefield NHP tells about a two-year war with Mexico. Washita Battlefield NHS tells the tragic aspects of U.S. westward expansion. Pueblos, cliff dwellings, and petroglyphs are reminders of the region's ancient civilizations.

Spend time exploring the contrasts of the Southwest Region and imagine its challenges for pioneers traveling the trails westward.

Did You Know?

- There are about 24,000 petroglyphs in Petroglyph NM in New Mexico. The ancestral Puebloan people etched the symbols into the rocks from 300 to 500 years ago.

- Padre Island NS on the coast of the Gulf of Mexico is the longest undeveloped stretch of barrier island in the world. Five of the world's seven species of sea turtles nest here.

- The limestone rock of Carlsbad Caverns holds ocean fossil plants and animals. Before the age of the dinosaurs, the southeastern corner of New Mexico was likely a coastline similar to the Florida Keys.

- There are more species of cactus at Big Bend NP in Texas than any other national park. Cacti usually bloom in April, which is a popular time to visit the park.

- The Cajun people of Louisiana came from western France by way of Acadie, Nova Scotia, in Canada. By the early 1800s, about 4,000 Acadians, later known as Cajuns, had settled in Louisiana. Learn about them at Jean Lafitte National Historical Park and Preserve.

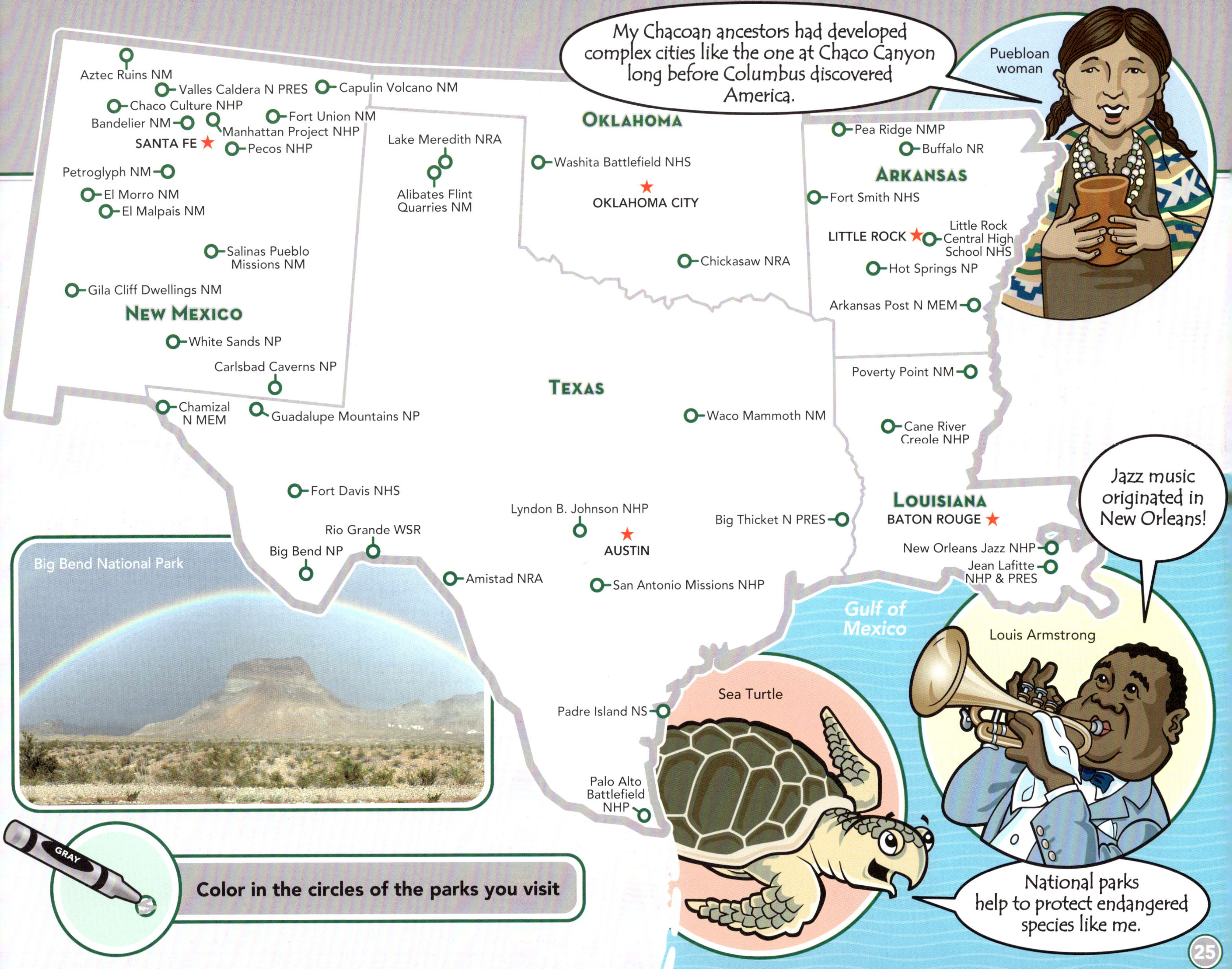

Color in the circles of the parks you visit

Parks that Explore Native American Cultures

Many parks preserve evidence of the first peoples to populate parts of what is now the United States. These include Native Americans, Alaska Natives, Native Hawaiians, and Pacific Islanders. Traditions and cultures of the native people still survive in many parts of the country. There are also parks that preserve remains of ancient civilizations that no longer exist. You'll find some of the most fascinating places to learn about Native American cultures when you visit these national park sites.

Native American Cultures
WORD FIND

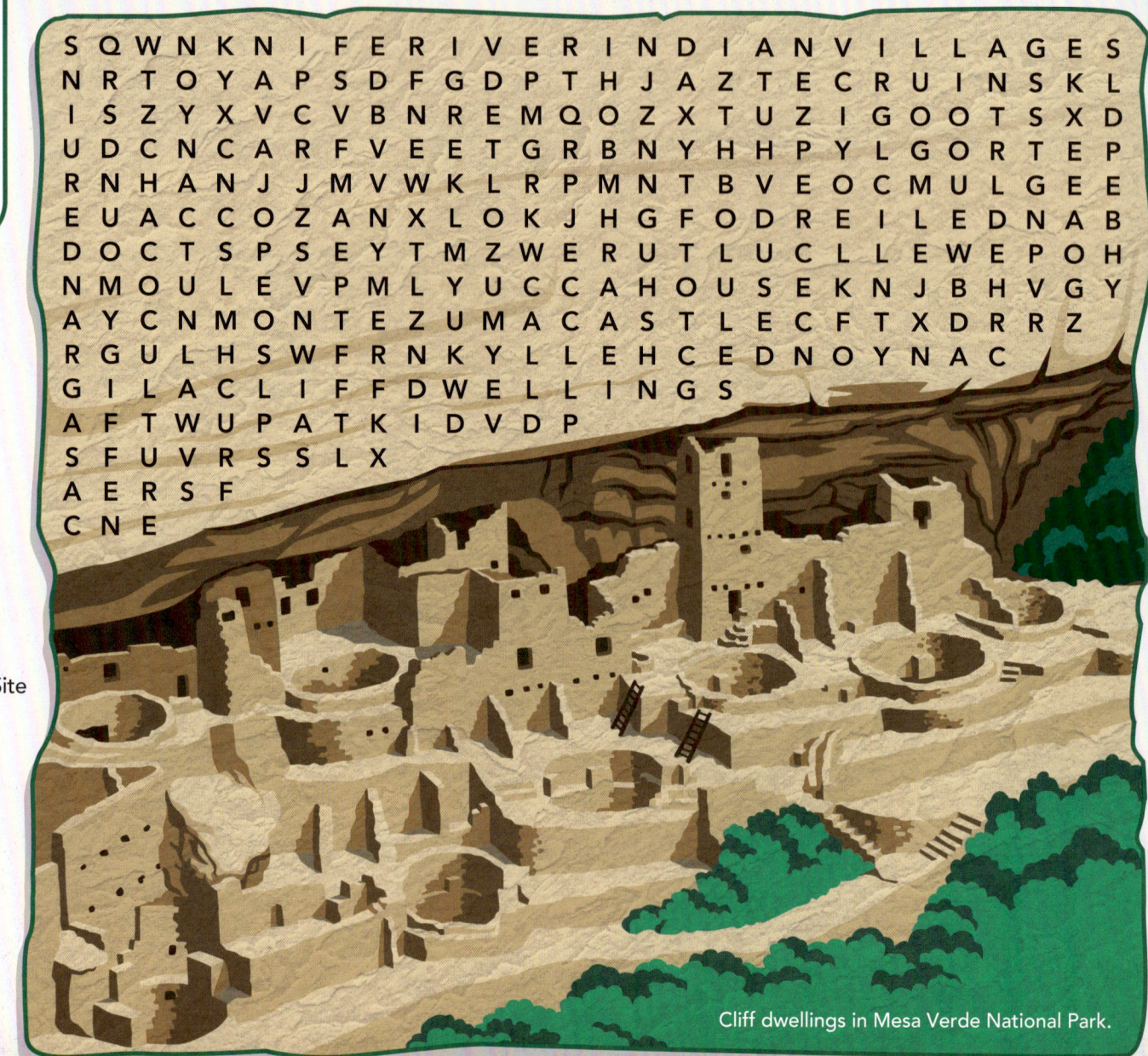

Can you find and circle the capitalized names of these parks? They are either up, down, across, or diagonal in the word find puzzle.

AZTEC RUINS National Monument
BANDELIER National Monument
CANYON DE CHELLY National Monument
CASA GRANDE RUINS National Monument
CHACO CULTURE National Historical Park
EFFIGY MOUNDS National Monument
EL MORRO National Monument
GILA CLIFF DWELLINGS National Monument
HOPEWELL CULTURE National Historical Park
HOVENWEEP National Monument
KNIFE RIVER INDIAN VILLAGES National Historic Site
MESA VERDE National Park
MONTEZUMA CASTLE National Monument
NAVAJO National Monument
NEZ PERCE National Historical Park
OCMULGEE National Monument
PETROGLYPH National Monument
TONTO National Monument
TUZIGOOT National Monument
WALNUT CANYON National Monument
WUPATKI National Monument
YUCCA HOUSE National Monument

```
S Q W N K N I F E R I V E R I N D I A N V I L L A G E S
N R T O Y A P S D F G D P T H J A Z T E C R U I N S K L
I S Z Y X V C V B N R E M Q O Z X T U Z I G O O T S X D
U D C N C A R F V E E T G R B N Y H H P Y L G O R T E P
R N H A N J J M V W K L R P M N T B V E O C M U L G E E
E U A C C O Z A N X L O K J H G F O D R E I L E D N A B
D O C T S P S E Y T M Z W E R U T L U C L L E W E P O H
N M O U L E V P M L Y U C C A H O U S E K N J B H V G Y
A Y C N M O N T E Z U M A C A S T L E C F T X D R R Z
R G U L H S W F R N K Y L L E H C E D N O Y N A C
G I L A C L I F F D W E L L I N G S
A F T W U P A T K I D V D P
S F U V R S S L X
A E R S F
C N E
```

Cliff dwellings in Mesa Verde National Park.

26

THEME: WESTWARD EXPANSION

Gateway Arch National Park

America Grows West

In today's world of high-speed transportation, it's hard to imagine what it was like to travel by wagon and foot across the vast western United States. The trip could take six months if you went all the way from the Missouri River to California or Oregon. But great waves of people did it in the 1840s, 1850s, and 1860s. They sought gold, oil, cattle, and farmland. Some followed the Mormon trail to religious freedom. Freedpeople sought homes of their own. Free land through the Homestead Act brought settlers from all walks of life to the Great Plains.

You can learn these stories and more at Nicodemus NHS, Homestead NHP, western forts, and along national historic trails that trace the migrations of people moving west for new opportunities. Try the scavenger hunt at Gateway Arch National Park in St. Louis to learn more about westward expansion. While there, be sure to take the tram to the top of the famous arch and look way out west. Imagine the courage it took to settle America's western frontier.

Photo of a homesteading family in the 1800s.

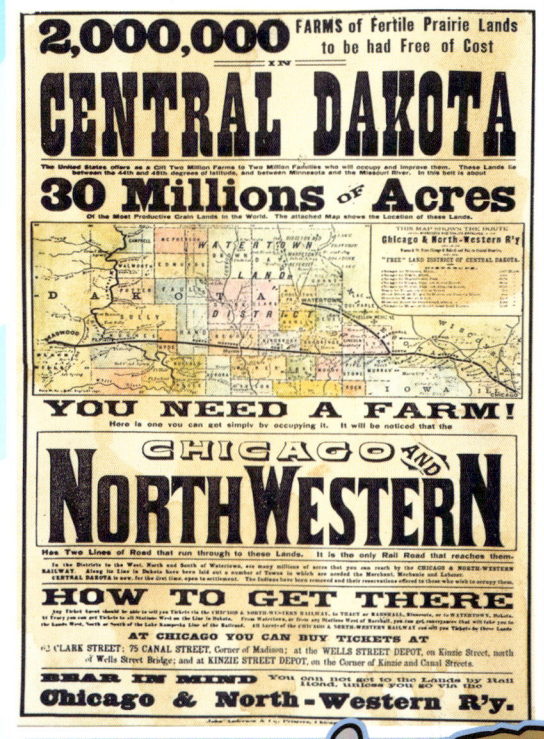

Poster encouraging people to settle in the west.

Rocky Mountain Region

DINO DIG Spot the Differences

These **STEGOSAURUS** skeletons may look the same at first glance, but there are 10 differences. Can you spot the differences by carefully comparing the top and bottom sets of bones?

National Parks in the Rocky Mountain Region

National parks in the Rocky Mountain Region have long been popular destinations for family vacations. Soon after Yellowstone became the world's first national park, railroads built lines to the parks and grand hotels for visitors. Automobiles increased access to the region's spectacular parks. Camping in Rocky Mountain NP; hiking in Glacier NP and Grand Teton NP; road trips through Arches, Canyonlands, and Zion national parks—you'll want to return again and again to enjoy the parks in this region.

You'll find interesting history here, too. See where railroads connected the continent at Golden Spike NHP. Learn about the 19th-century cattle industry at Grant-Kohrs Ranch NHS. See how Native Americans once lived at Mesa Verde and Hovenweep.

There's no end to variety in Rocky Mountain parks!

Did You Know?

- The quarry at Dinosaur NM in Colorado has more Jurassic dinosaur remains than anywhere else in the world.

- The cliff dwellings at Mesa Verde NP are made from sandstone, mortar, and wood beams. The Cliff Palace was an ancient apartment building with 150 rooms!

- Yellowstone NP contains one of the world's largest active volcanoes. The park has more than 300 geysers, including Old Faithful, which spews water and steam high into the air about every 90 minutes.

- Natural Bridges NM is the world's first International Dark Sky Park. On a clear night you can see the Milky Way galaxy and countless stars and planets overlooking Natural Bridges.

- Ouch! The surface temperature of the sand at Great Sand Dunes NP can reach over 140°, so wear shoes when you hike there.

- The colorful rock spires of Bryce Canyon NP are called "hoodoos." They were formed by ice and water wearing away weak limestone.

Can you color in this Stegosaurus? What color do you think the Stegosaurus was? Do you think it had spots or stripes?

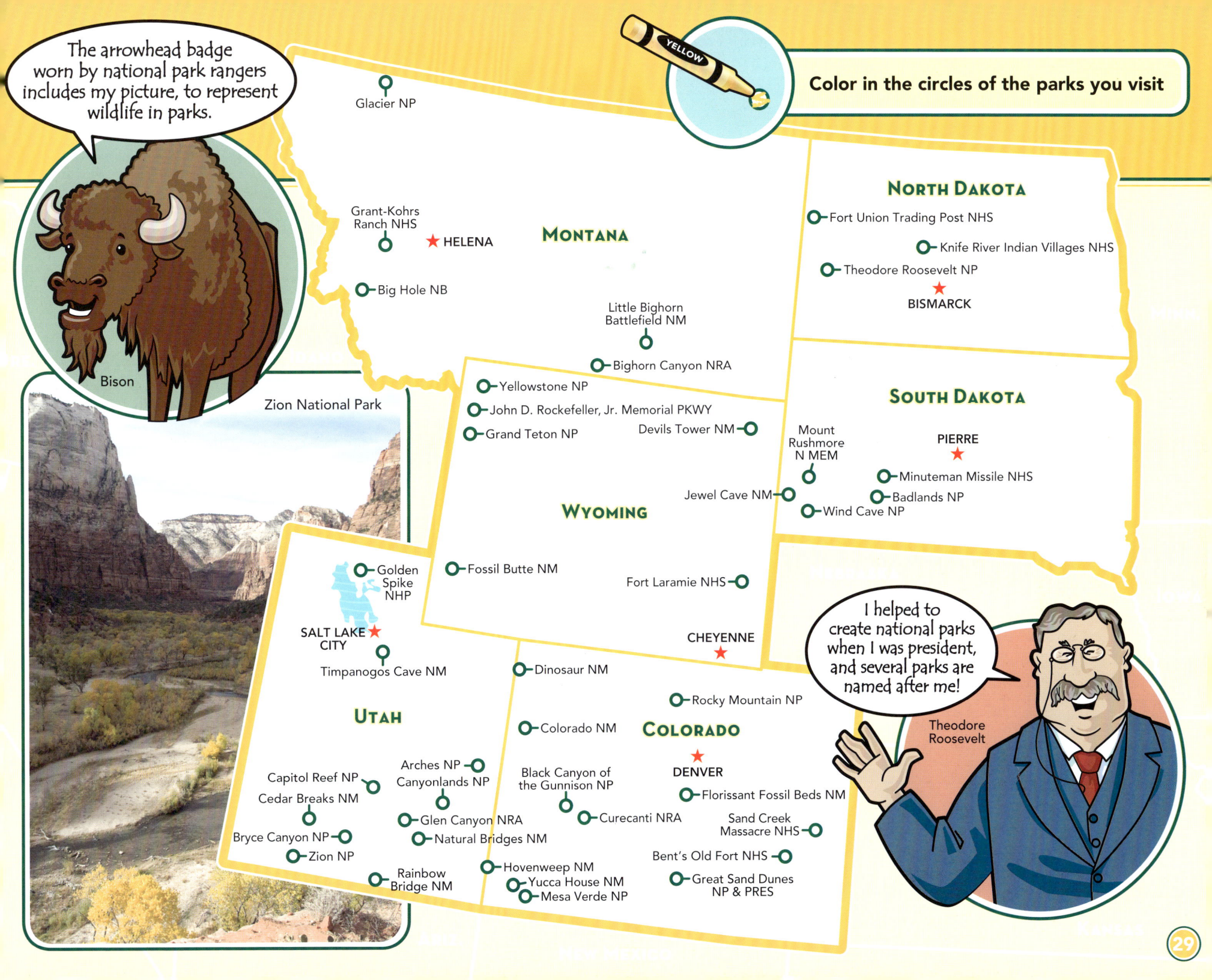

The arrowhead badge worn by national park rangers includes my picture, to represent wildlife in parks.

Bison

Color in the circles of the parks you visit

Montana
- Glacier NP
- Grant-Kohrs Ranch NHS
- ★ HELENA
- Big Hole NB
- Little Bighorn Battlefield NM
- Bighorn Canyon NRA

North Dakota
- Fort Union Trading Post NHS
- Knife River Indian Villages NHS
- Theodore Roosevelt NP
- ★ BISMARCK

South Dakota
- Mount Rushmore N MEM
- ★ PIERRE
- Minuteman Missile NHS
- Jewel Cave NM
- Badlands NP
- Wind Cave NP

Wyoming
- Yellowstone NP
- John D. Rockefeller, Jr. Memorial PKWY
- Grand Teton NP
- Devils Tower NM
- Fossil Butte NM
- Fort Laramie NHS
- ★ CHEYENNE

Zion National Park

Utah
- Golden Spike NHP
- ★ SALT LAKE CITY
- Timpanogos Cave NM
- Capitol Reef NP
- Arches NP
- Canyonlands NP
- Cedar Breaks NM
- Glen Canyon NRA
- Bryce Canyon NP
- Natural Bridges NM
- Zion NP
- Rainbow Bridge NM

Colorado
- Dinosaur NM
- Rocky Mountain NP
- Colorado NM
- Black Canyon of the Gunnison NP
- ★ DENVER
- Florissant Fossil Beds NM
- Curecanti NRA
- Sand Creek Massacre NHS
- Hovenweep NM
- Bent's Old Fort NHS
- Yucca House NM
- Mesa Verde NP
- Great Sand Dunes NP & PRES

I helped to create national parks when I was president, and several parks are named after me!

Theodore Roosevelt

29

SEARCH FOR WILDLIFE

When visiting nature parks, it's fun to see how many birds and animals you can find. Some people keep lists of all the wildlife they see while exploring. It helps to have binoculars with you so you can see the animals up close without disturbing them. **Remember: for your safety and for the good of the animals, don't get too close—and never feed wildlife.**

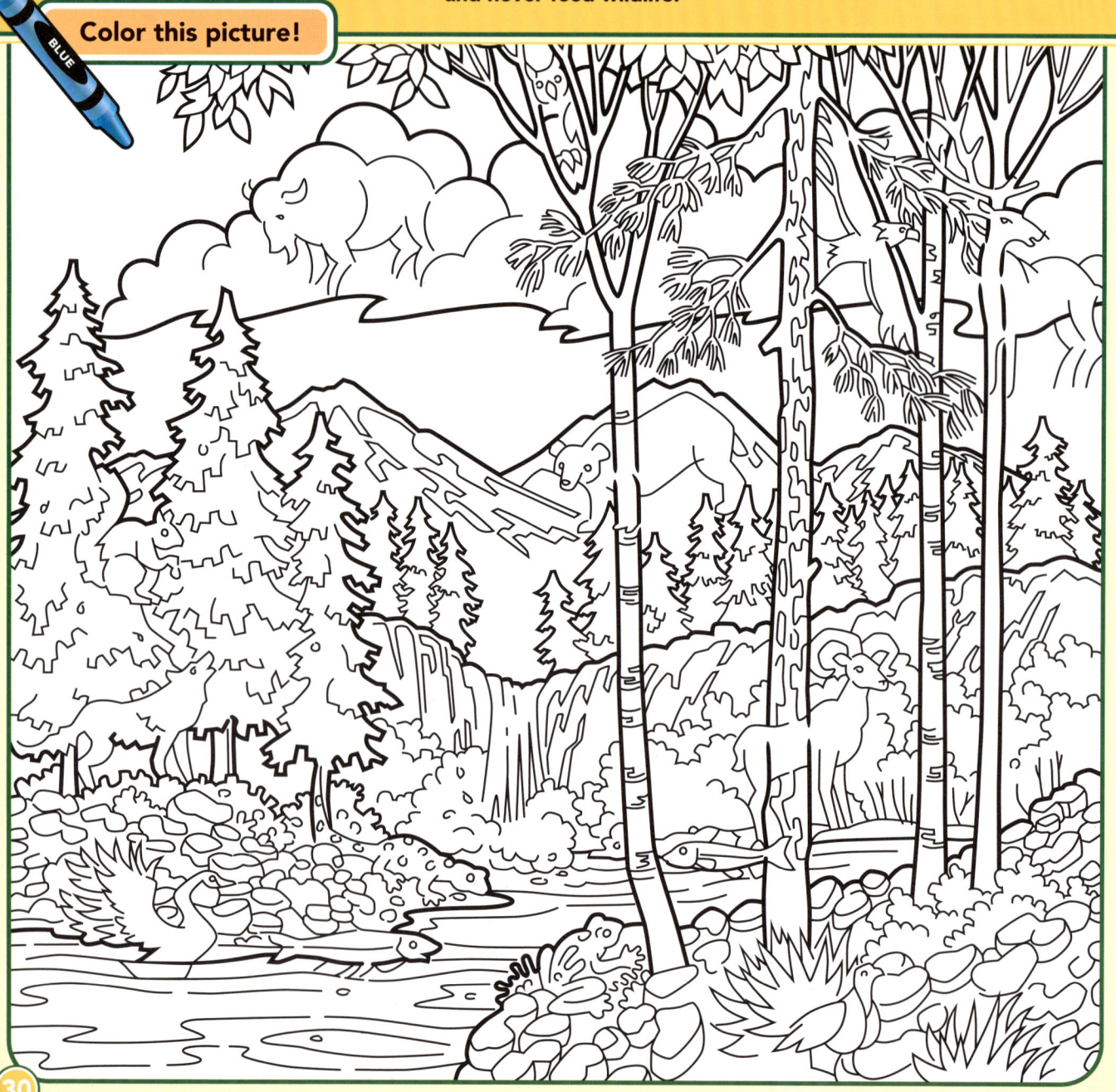

Color this picture!

Enjoy searching for these creatures that you might spot if you were to hike through Rocky Mountain National Park, Grand Teton National Park, or Yellowstone National Park. **In the picture to the left, can you find:**

- BALD EAGLE
- BOREAL CHORUS FROG
- BIGHORN RAM
- BISON
- BLACK BEAR
- ELK
- GREAT HORNED OWL
- GRAY WOLF
- LONGNOSE DACE
- SAGE GROUSE
- MOUNTAIN WHITEFISH
- RED SQUIRREL
- TIGER SALAMANDER
- TRUMPETER SWAN

THEME: Nature's Wonders

America's Amazing Treasures

America's national parks hold some of nature's most amazing creations. People come from all over the world to see Old Faithful and the thousands of other thermal features at Yellowstone. Rainbow Bridge—the world's largest natural bridge—and more than 2,000 natural arches at Arches NP are among the other attractions of this region. Grand Canyon to the west is one of the seven "Natural Wonders of the World." White Sands NP in New Mexico is part of the world's largest gypsum desert. To the east, Mammoth Cave in Kentucky is the world's longest recorded cave.

But natural wonders don't need to break world records to inspire awe. Every region has extraordinary things to see in its natural parks. Sometimes the most amazing natural wonders are the smallest. The diverse organisms and systems that sustain the natural environment are amazing, too.

Arches National Park

White Sands National Park

Old Faithful, Yellowstone National Park

Mammoth Cave National Park

Nature's Treasures Crossword

Western Region

Across

4. If you are not afraid of anything, you are _____.
5. Coldest season.
6. San Francisco and Las Vegas are both _____.
8. Another word for a thought.
9. U.S. state where Great Basin National Park is located.
10. Cone-shaped rock formation that can erupt.
12. When it _____, it pours!
15. What spews out of a volcano.
16. Between a ____ and a hard place.
17. Channel _____ National Park, in California.
19. Area with a lot of trees.
21. Season when flowers bloom.
23. U.S. state that is a group of islands in the Pacific Ocean.
26. Where you go to learn.
27. Season that is hot and sunny.
28. Go and _____ the national parks!

Down

1. Tallest type of trees.
2. Famous national park in Arizona.
3. Death Valley National Park is mostly a _____.
7. Winter, spring, summer, and fall are the four _____.
11. U.S. state where the Grand Canyon is located.
13. Season when leaves change colors.
14. U.S. state where Yosemite National Park is located.
18. The world of living things and the outdoors.
20. Valuable things worth keeping.
22. Brisk walk along a nature trail.
24. Environmentalist who has a national park named after him in California.
25. Famous national park that is located in California.

National Parks in the Western Region

You can see nature's extremes in the parks of the Western Region. Visit Death Valley NP, one of the lowest, hottest, driest places on Earth, and learn how species have adapted to survive extreme conditions. See giant cacti at Saguaro NP, some as tall as 50 feet and weighing 10 tons. At Sequoia NP and Kings Canyon NP you'll see huge sequoia trees, the largest living things on Earth. At Muir Woods NM you'll see some of the world's tallest trees. At Yosemite NP, see the highest waterfall in North America.

Nature has other surprises for you, too. Learn how geologic forces created the features you see at Lassen Volcanic NP, Pinnacles NP, and Devils Postpile NM. Visit the world's most massive volcano at Hawai'i Volcanoes NP.

Western Region parks are also rich with human history. Cliff dwellings reveal ancient civilizations. You can learn about Indians still living in this region at Canyon de Chelly NM. If you venture to Hawaii, you'll learn about Pacific Islanders. Parks in the Pacific also tell the complex stories of world war.

You'll have an extremely good time discovering parks in the Western Region.

Did You Know?

The largest tree in the world is named the General Sherman and is at Sequoia NP. It measures 102 feet around at its base and is nearly 275 feet tall.

World War II was the most destructive war in history and involved more than 60 countries. The U.S. entered the war in 1941 after Japan attacked the navy fleet at Pearl Harbor, Hawaii. At the USS *Arizona* Memorial you can see the underwater wreckage of the battleship sunk in that attack.

At Golden Gate NRA you can ride a ferryboat to Alcatraz Island to visit its famous prison and learn how people lived on the island—inside and outside the prison walls.

In this region of extremes, you can stand atop Mount Whitney in California—the highest point in the lower 48 states—and look down on the lowest point—Death Valley.

Yosemite NP is actually older than Yellowstone NP as a public park. Yosemite was set aside in 1864, but at the time it was administered by the State of California. It became a national park in 1890, 18 years after Yellowstone.

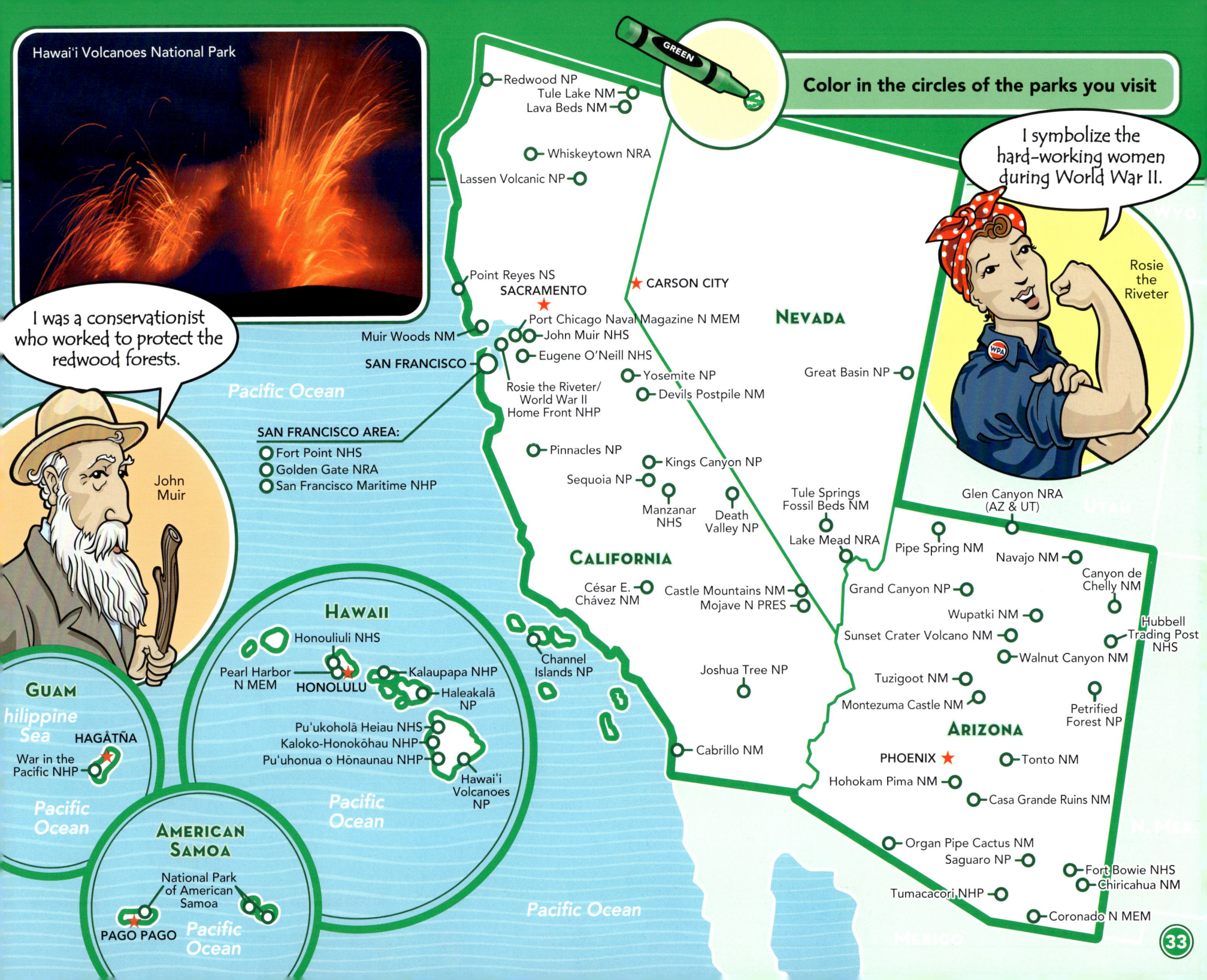

Hawai'i Volcanoes National Park

Color in the circles of the parks you visit

"I was a conservationist who worked to protect the redwood forests." — **John Muir**

"I symbolize the hard-working women during World War II." — **Rosie the Riveter**

California
- Redwood NP
- Tule Lake NM
- Lava Beds NM
- Whiskeytown NRA
- Lassen Volcanic NP
- Point Reyes NS
- Muir Woods NM
- Port Chicago Naval Magazine N MEM
- John Muir NHS
- Eugene O'Neill NHS
- Rosie the Riveter/World War II Home Front NHP
- Yosemite NP
- Devils Postpile NM
- Pinnacles NP
- Kings Canyon NP
- Sequoia NP
- Manzanar NHS
- Death Valley NP
- César E. Chávez NM
- Castle Mountains NM
- Mojave N PRES
- Joshua Tree NP
- Channel Islands NP
- Cabrillo NM

SACRAMENTO ★
SAN FRANCISCO

SAN FRANCISCO AREA:
- Fort Point NHS
- Golden Gate NRA
- San Francisco Maritime NHP

Nevada
- Great Basin NP
- Tule Springs Fossil Beds NM
- Lake Mead NRA

CARSON CITY ★

Arizona
- Glen Canyon NRA (AZ & UT)
- Pipe Spring NM
- Navajo NM
- Canyon de Chelly NM
- Grand Canyon NP
- Wupatki NM
- Hubbell Trading Post NHS
- Sunset Crater Volcano NM
- Walnut Canyon NM
- Tuzigoot NM
- Montezuma Castle NM
- Petrified Forest NP
- Tonto NM
- Hohokam Pima NM
- Casa Grande Ruins NM
- Organ Pipe Cactus NM
- Saguaro NP
- Fort Bowie NHS
- Chiricahua NM
- Tumacácori NHP
- Coronado N MEM

PHOENIX ★

Hawaii
- Honouliuli NHS
- Pearl Harbor N MEM
- Kalaupapa NHP
- Haleakalā NP
- Pu'ukoholā Heiau NHS
- Kaloko-Honokōhau NHP
- Pu'uhonua o Hōnaunau NHP
- Hawai'i Volcanoes NP

HONOLULU

Guam
- War in the Pacific NHP

HAGÅTÑA

American Samoa
- National Park of American Samoa

PAGO PAGO

33

GRAND CANYON MAZE

Can you find a path through the maze, from the top of the canyon down to the bottom where the Colorado River flows?

START

END

Grand Canyon National Park is one of the most popular parks in America. The canyon was formed by the action of the Colorado River slowly grinding away the rocks to form a canyon that is 277 miles long and over a mile deep in some places. Visitors come from all over the world for the awe-inspiring views and to enjoy hiking the trails, rafting on the river, or riding slowly down the canyon and back on a mule.

THEME: Seashores & Lakeshores

Point Reyes National Seashore
Photo by Miguel Vieira

Cape Lookout National Seashore

Apostle Islands National Lakeshore

Padre Island National Seashore

Angelfish

Roseate tern

America's Best Beaches

America is a beautiful country "from sea to shining sea." And some of the prettiest places are its national seashores and lakeshores. There are 10 national seashores: seven along the Atlantic Coast, two along the Gulf of Mexico, and one on the Pacific Coast. Three national lakeshores border the Great Lakes. See if you can find all the places with NS (for national seashore) and NL (for national lakeshore) on the regional maps in this book. You might spot other parks on the water too, like Dry Tortugas and Virgin Islands national parks, which also have beautiful beaches.

National parks protect these beaches so that everyone can enjoy them. Look further when you visit waterfront parks and you'll learn other reasons why national seashores and lakeshores are important. They protect the homes of many rare and endangered species. They also protect artifacts that tell America's maritime history of shipwrecks and pirates, military actions, and coastal navigation.

Come get your feet wet at America's national seashores, lakeshores, and other waterfront parks.

Wild horse and egret at Assateague Island National Seashore.

35

Draw a Totem Pole

Pacific Northwest & Alaska Region

National Parks in the Pacific Northwest & Alaska Region

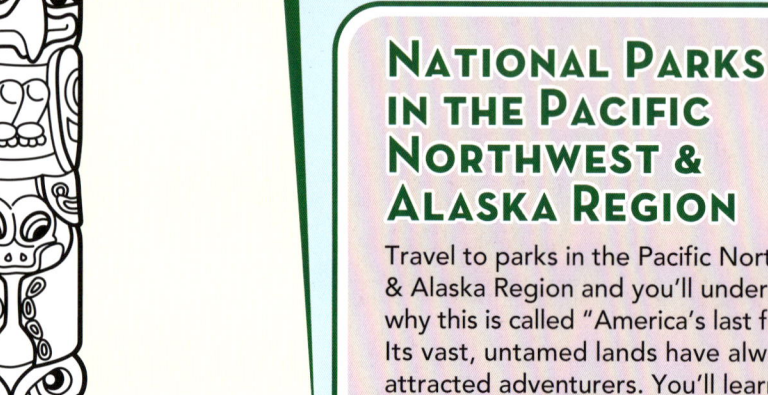

Travel to parks in the Pacific Northwest & Alaska Region and you'll understand why this is called "America's last frontier." Its vast, untamed lands have always attracted adventurers. You'll learn about them at Fort Vancouver, Klondike Gold Rush, and other historical parks. At Sitka NHP, you'll learn about clashes between Alaska Natives and Russians. At San Juan Island NHP, you'll learn how the U.S. and Great Britain nearly went to war over a pig!

But it is in the wild beauty of its nature parks where this region excels. One eye-popping scene after another unfolds at Pacific Northwest & Alaskan parks. At places like Craters of the Moon and Aniakchak, you'll learn what forces of nature created this region's stunning landscapes.

Wherever your adventures take you in the Pacific Northwest & Alaska Region, expect to be "wowed."

Did You Know?

Hagerman Fossil Beds NM is one of the best places in the world for scientists to study fossils of horses. More than 200 partial and 30 complete skeletons, estimated to be 3 to 4 million years old, have been found there.

Lewis and Clark reached their destination and first saw the Pacific Ocean from Cape Disappointment at the mouth of the Columbia River. They later crossed the Columbia and camped for the winter at Fort Clatsop.

Mount Rainier is an active volcano. It last erupted 150 years ago. Scientists have installed special sensor equipment to detect signs if it is ready to erupt again—in time to warn people to move to safety.

During the Yukon Gold Rush of 1897, prospectors had to travel hundreds of miles on foot over hard Alaskan terrain, carrying the gear they would need in the gold fields. Most were disappointed when they arrived to find that the best claims had already been staked. The rush was over by 1899.

Crater Lake is 1,943 feet deep—the deepest lake in the United States. It is also thought to be the clearest lake in the world.

Totem poles are large sculptures carved from tall trees by the native people of the Pacific Northwest coast and Alaska. Some totem poles tell a story, with the characters stacked in a vertical row from top to bottom. Other totem poles show family groups. Totems were used in funerals and other ceremonies or for artistic decoration.

Here's an example of a totem pole you can color. In the space beside it, draw your own totem pole. Will yours include animals and birds or people, such as your friends or family?

Alaska

- Cape Krusenstern NM
- Noatak N PRES
- Kobuk Valley NP
- Gates of the Arctic NP & PRES
- Bering Land Bridge N PRES
- Yukon-Charley Rivers N PRES
- Denali NP & PRES
- Lake Clark NP & PRES
- Alagnak Wild River
- Wrangell-St. Elias NP & PRES
- Katmai NP & PRES
- Kenai Fjords NP
- Aniakchak NM & PRES
- Glacier Bay NP & PRES
- Klondike Gold Rush NHP
- ★ JUNEAU
- Sitka NHP

"Lots of people come up to Alaska to fish for me!" — Salmon

Crater Lake National Park

Washington

- San Juan Island NHP
- North Cascades NP
- Ross Lake NRA
- Ebey's Landing NH RES
- Olympic NP
- Lake Chelan NRA
- ★ OLYMPIA
- Klondike Gold Rush NHP
- Lake Roosevelt NRA
- Mount Rainier NP
- Manhattan Project NHP
- Lewis & Clark NHP
- Fort Vancouver NHS
- Whitman Mission NHS
- Nez Perce NHP

Oregon

- ★ SALEM
- John Day Fossil Beds NM
- Crater Lake NP
- Oregon Caves NM & PRES

Idaho

- ★ BOISE
- Craters of the Moon NM & PRES
- Hagerman Fossil Beds NM
- Minidoka NHS
- City of Rocks N RES

"I helped to guide Lewis and Clark across the wild west!" — Sacagawea, Lemhi Shoshone guide

"We took the first expedition to the Pacific Coast and back." — Meriwether Lewis, William Clark

Color in the circles of the parks you visit

37

Purple Mountains Majesty

America's mountains have stories to tell. The distinct mountain ranges that characterize the eastern and western parts of the country and a few interior places are the results of ancient geologic forces. The eastern mountains are much older and more worn down than peaks in the West.

Mountains define watersheds, types of soils and rocks, what plants grow there or not, what animals live there or not. Mountains influence weather, water supplies, population, and economics.

For much of U.S. history, mountains were barriers that affected transportation, commerce, and even politics. There are national parks that tell the stories of the mountains—places like Great Smoky Mountains, Cumberland Gap, Guadalupe Mountains, Wrangell-St. Elias, Denali, and Hawai'i Volcanoes.

Modern roads make it possible for us to cross over or pass through mountains easily today. No longer the obstacles they once were, mountains attract travelers to their beautiful scenery and outdoor recreation. When you see that a park is located in mountainous terrain, you can be sure it will have places to hike, climb, camp, view wildlife and scenic wonders and, yes, learn the stories to be told in those highlands.

The differences between mountains in the eastern and western U.S. tell a lot about how this part of the world evolved. Explore America's majestic mountains. There is always something new to discover.

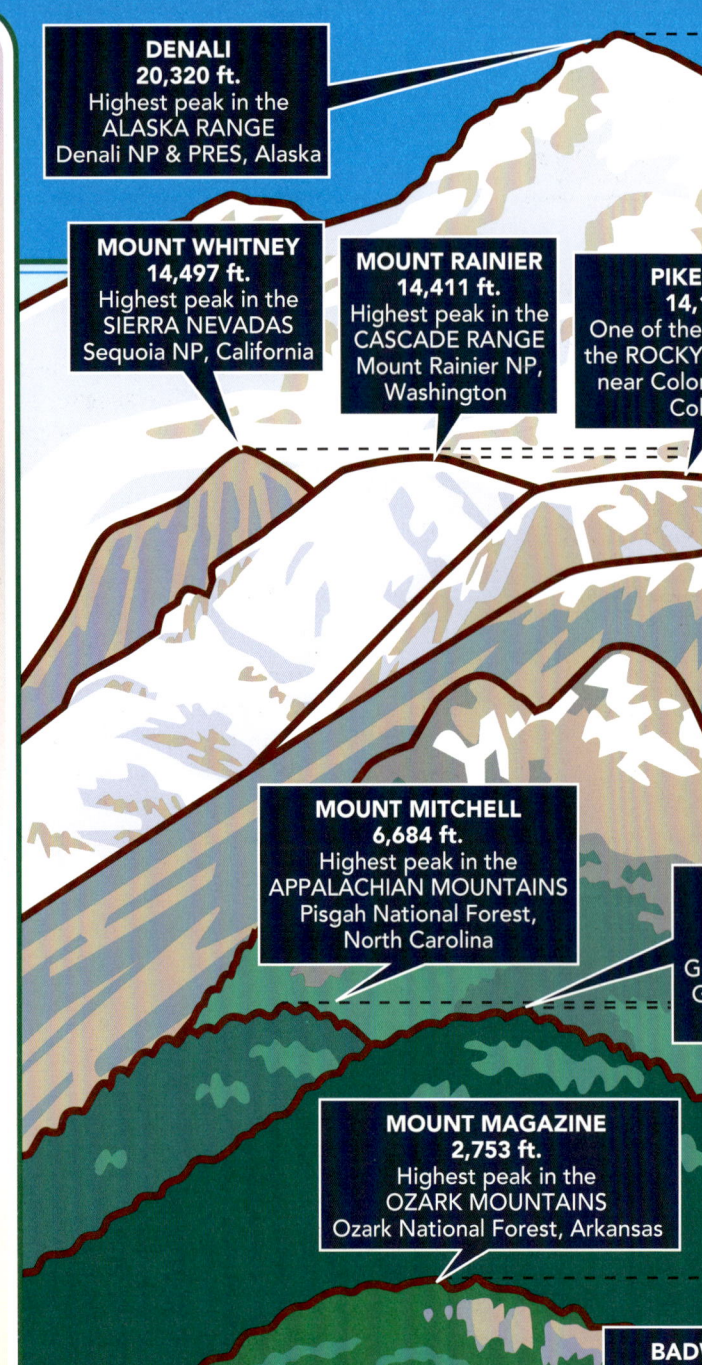

DENALI 20,320 ft. Highest peak in the ALASKA RANGE — Denali NP & PRES, Alaska

MOUNT WHITNEY 14,497 ft. Highest peak in the SIERRA NEVADAS — Sequoia NP, California

MOUNT RAINIER 14,411 ft. Highest peak in the CASCADE RANGE — Mount Rainier NP, Washington

PIKES PEAK 14,115 ft. One of the high peaks in the ROCKY MOUNTAINS near Colorado Springs, Colorado

MAUNA KEA 13,796 ft. Highest peak in HAWAII — Hawai'i Volcanoes NP, Hawaii

GRAND TETON 13,770 ft. Highest peak in the TETON RANGE — Grand Teton NP, Wyoming

MOUNT MITCHELL 6,684 ft. Highest peak in the APPALACHIAN MOUNTAINS — Pisgah National Forest, North Carolina

CLINGMANS DOME 6,643 ft. Highest peak in the GREAT SMOKY MOUNTAINS — Great Smoky Mountains NP, Tennessee

MOUNT MAGAZINE 2,753 ft. Highest peak in the OZARK MOUNTAINS — Ozark National Forest, Arkansas

BADWATER BASIN 282 ft. below sea level — Lowest point in the U.S. Death Valley NP, California

THEME: Recreational Sites

What Can You Do at a National Park?

The short answer is "plenty." America's national parks are great places for having fun. The very first national park, Yellowstone, was set aside "as a public park or pleasuring ground for the benefit and enjoyment of the people." Nearly every national park created since includes recreation as part of its purpose.

There are 18 national recreation areas set aside primarily as places for outdoor play. They include lakes, rivers, and large urban parks, like Golden Gate NRA and Boston Harbor Islands NRA. Parks of all types and sizes in every region offer wonderful ways to play. How about sledding and sandboarding at Great Sand Dunes NP in Colorado or skiing and snowboarding at Yosemite NP in California? There are places for snorkeling, kayaking, fishing, and other water activities, and also places to hike, bike, and camp.

Whether looking for a new place to enjoy your favorite activities, or a place to try something new, get out and enjoy your national parks.

Hiking along the Lewis and Clark National Historic Trail.

Bikers resting along Big South Fork National River & Recreation Area.

Activity Checklist

Symbols like the ones pictured here are used on park signs and publications to identify activities you can do there. Can you match the activity below with its symbol?

- HIKING
- CANOEING
- HORSEBACK RIDING
- SWIMMING
- BIKING
- CAMPING
- PICNICKING
- SKIING
- ICE-SKATING

Passport® Cancellation Stamps

Whenever you visit a national park, you can get a free Passport To Your National Parks® cancellation stamp at the park's visitor center. These circular ink stamps record the name of the park and the date of your visit.
Use these pages to collect as many cancellation stamps as you can!

Here is an example of a park cancellation stamp.

Ranger Autographs

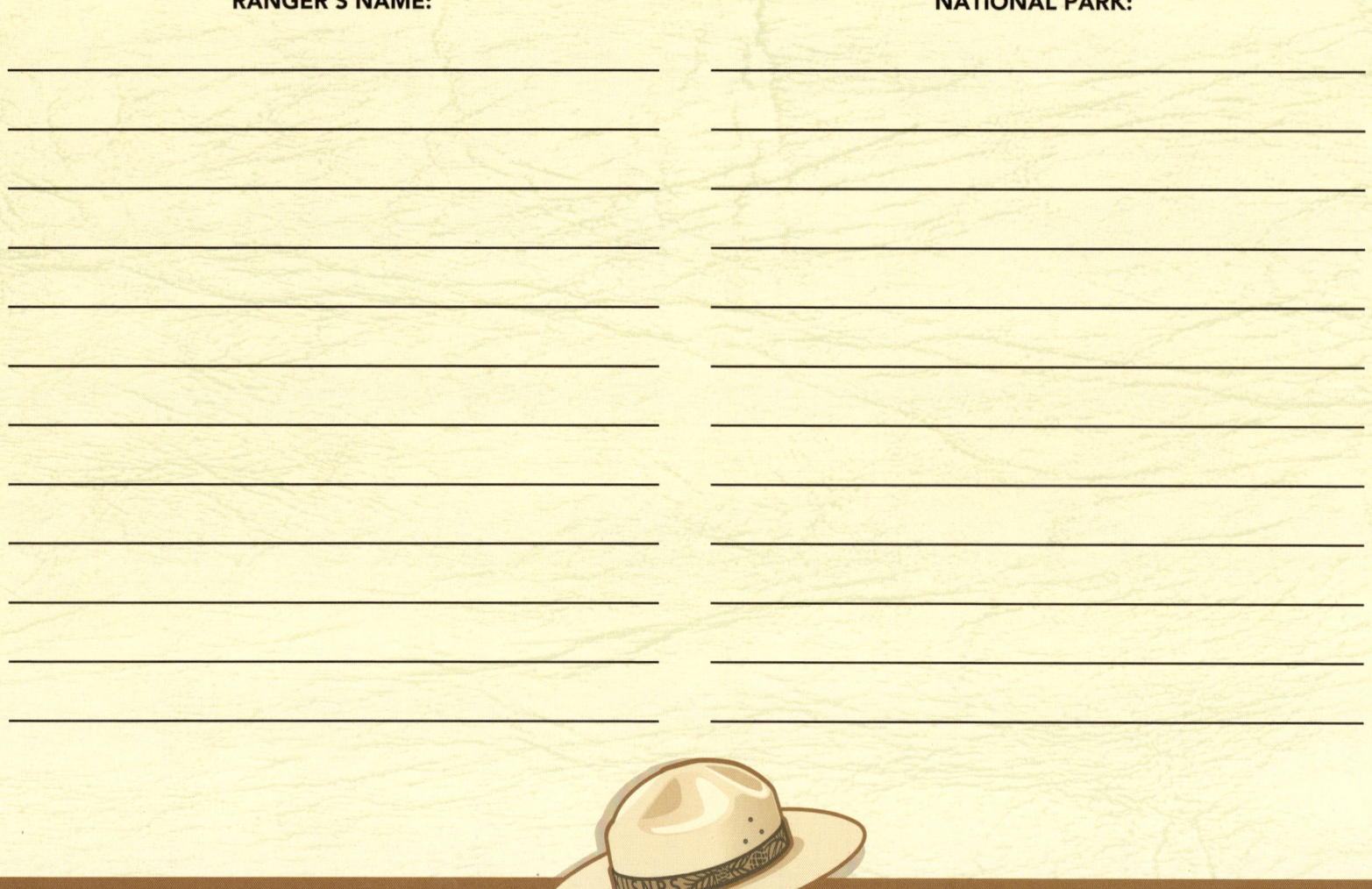

Rangers work in the parks to help visitors like you. How many rangers have you met?

RANGER'S NAME: **NATIONAL PARK:**

My Journal Page

Use this page to jot down your favorite memories when you travel to the national parks.

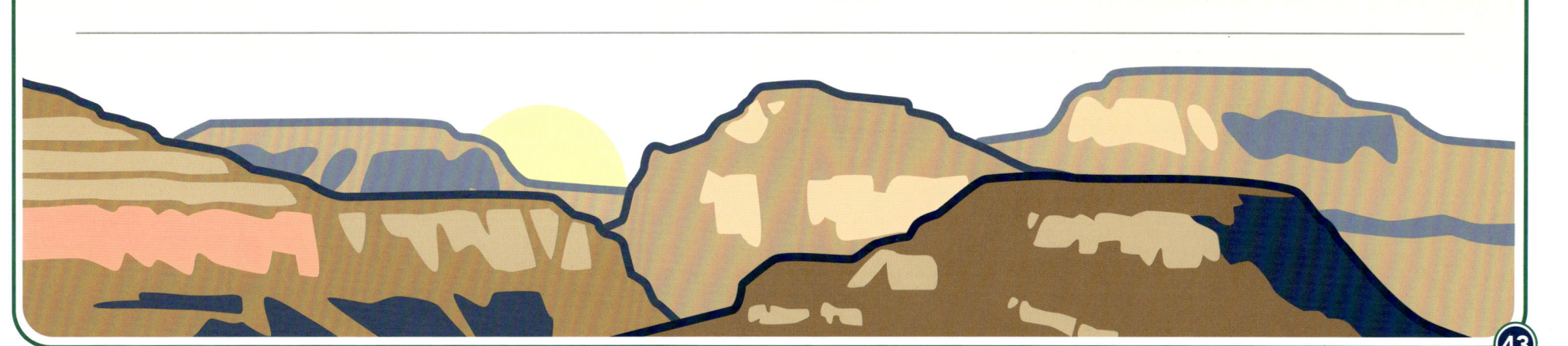

My Memories

Use these pages to draw your favorite national park or paste in some of your favorite photos.

Answers to Mazes,
Climb the Steps of the Lincoln Memorial

Maze of Liberty
Page 4

Find the Differences
Page 12

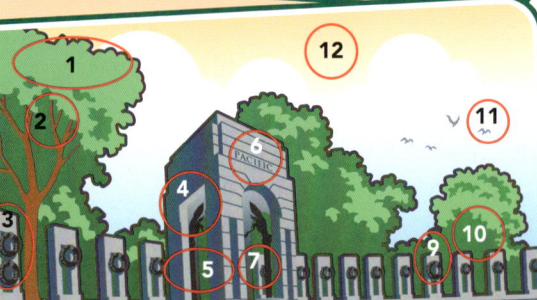

12 Differences:
1–leaf detail on upper left tree is missing, 2–extra tree branch, 3–two wreaths on far left stand, 4–left archway is squared-off instead of round, 5–missing extra windows on either side of left arch, 6–"Pacific" instead of "Atlantic," 7–extra wreath stand seen through right archway, 8–higher water sprays in fountain, 9–larger wreath on right side, 10–right side tree trunk is missing, 11–extra bird in sky, 12–sky color has changed.

Liberty Bell Word Find
Page 8

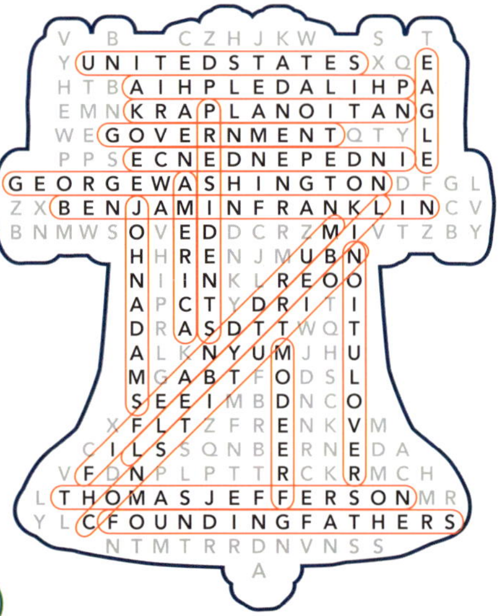

Page 14

Whew! All those steps have made me tired. I think I will sit down and rest a while.

5. What U.S. coin has a picture of the Lincoln Memorial?
The penny.

4. Who served the shortest term as U.S. president?
William Henry Harrison died of pneumonia in 1841 after only one month as president.

3. At what national park site can you see the clothes that President Abraham Lincoln wore the night he was shot?
Ford's Theatre NHS in Washington, D.C.

2. Three U.S. presidents died on the Fourth of July. Can you name them?
1. *John Adams died on July 4, 1826, the nation's 50th birthday.*
2. *Thomas Jefferson also died on July 4, 1826.*
3. *James Monroe died July 4, 1831.*

1. Six parks are associated with President Theodore Roosevelt, including Mount Rushmore N MEM and his home at Sagamore Hill. Can you name the other four parks?
1. *Theodore Roosevelt National Park*
2. *Theodore Roosevelt Island*
3. *Theodore Roosevelt Birthplace NHS*
4. *Theodore Roosevelt Inaugural NHS*

Southeast Forts Crossword Puzzle
Page 18

PUZZLES, AND GAMES

CONNECT the DOTS
Page 16

It's an alligator!

START HERE

First Ladies MATCH GAME
Page 20

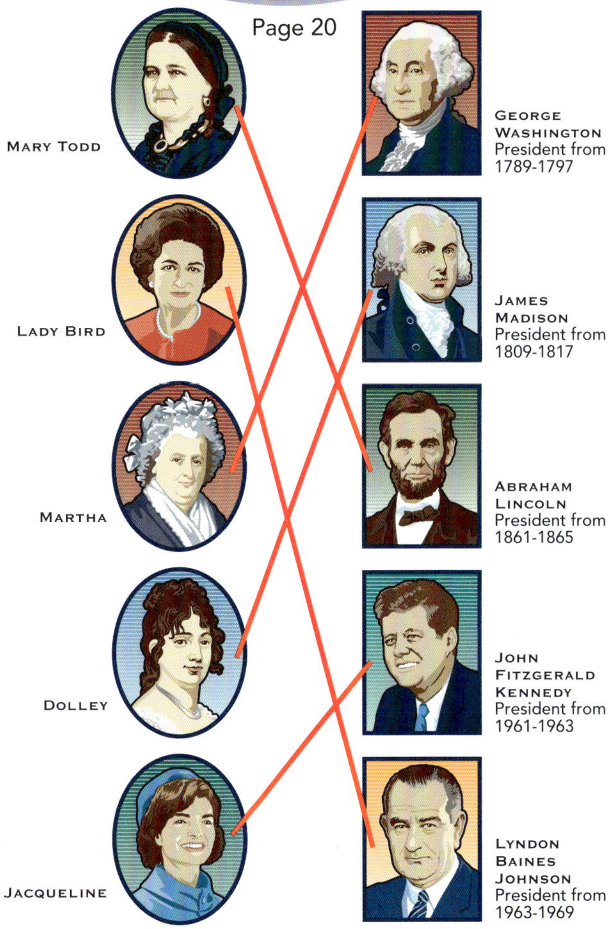

- Mary Todd — Abraham Lincoln, President from 1861-1865
- Lady Bird — Lyndon Baines Johnson, President from 1963-1969
- Martha — George Washington, President from 1789-1797
- Dolley — James Madison, President from 1809-1817
- Jacqueline — John Fitzgerald Kennedy, President from 1961-1963

Voyageurs Waterways
Page 22

START → END

Abraham Lincoln
Page 21

1. Lincoln Memorial
2. Abraham Lincoln Birthplace NHP
3. Lincoln Boyhood N MEM
4. Lincoln Home NHS

MOUNT RUSHMORE   Page 15
Can you name the four presidents who appear on Mt. Rushmore?

1. George Washington
2. Thomas Jefferson
3. Theodore Roosevelt
4. Abraham Lincoln

Famous Americans   Page 23

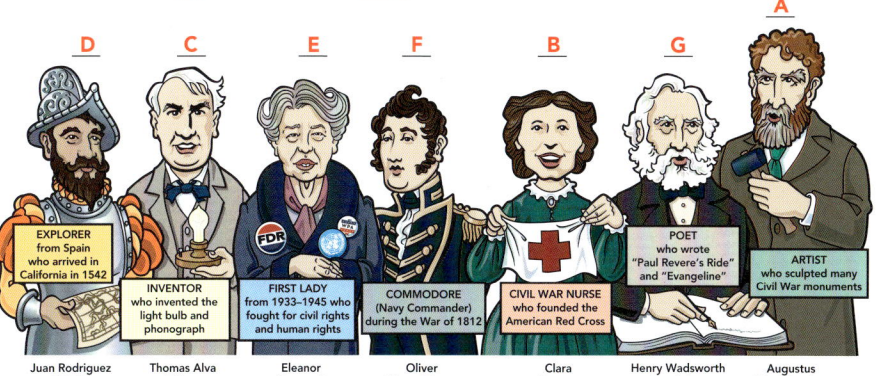

- **A** — ARTIST who sculpted many Civil War monuments — Augustus Saint-Gaudens
- **B** — CIVIL WAR NURSE who founded the American Red Cross — Clara Barton
- **C** — INVENTOR who invented the light bulb and phonograph — Thomas Alva Edison
- **D** — EXPLORER from Spain who arrived in California in 1542 — Juan Rodriguez Cabrillo
- **E** — FIRST LADY from 1933–1945 who fought for civil rights and human rights — Eleanor Roosevelt
- **F** — COMMODORE (Navy Commander) during the War of 1812 — Oliver Hazard Perry
- **G** — POET who wrote "Paul Revere's Ride" and "Evangeline" — Henry Wadsworth Longfellow

47

Native American Cultures Word Find
Page 26

```
S Q W N K N I F E R I V E R I N D I A N V I L L A G E S
N R T O Y A P S D F G D P T H J A Z T E C R U I N S K L
I S D Z N X C V B N R E M O O Z X T U Z I G O O T S X D
U C Z N C A R F V E E T R B N Y H P Y L G O R T E P A
R H N A N J J M V W K F P M N T B V E O C M U L G E E
E A O C O Z N X L O K J H G F D R E I L E D N A B X
D C M U S P S E Y T M Z W E R U T L U C L L E W E P O H
N O Y T L E V P M L Y U C C A H O U S E K N J B H V G Y
A M N M O N T E Z U M A C A S T L E C F T X D R R Z
R A G U L H S W F R N K Y L L E H C E D N O Y N A C
G Y C G I L A C L I F F D W E L L I N G S
I A S U T W U P A T K I D V D P
L F F E F U V R S S L X
A S C E N S F
C
```

Dino Dig — Spot the Differences
Page 28

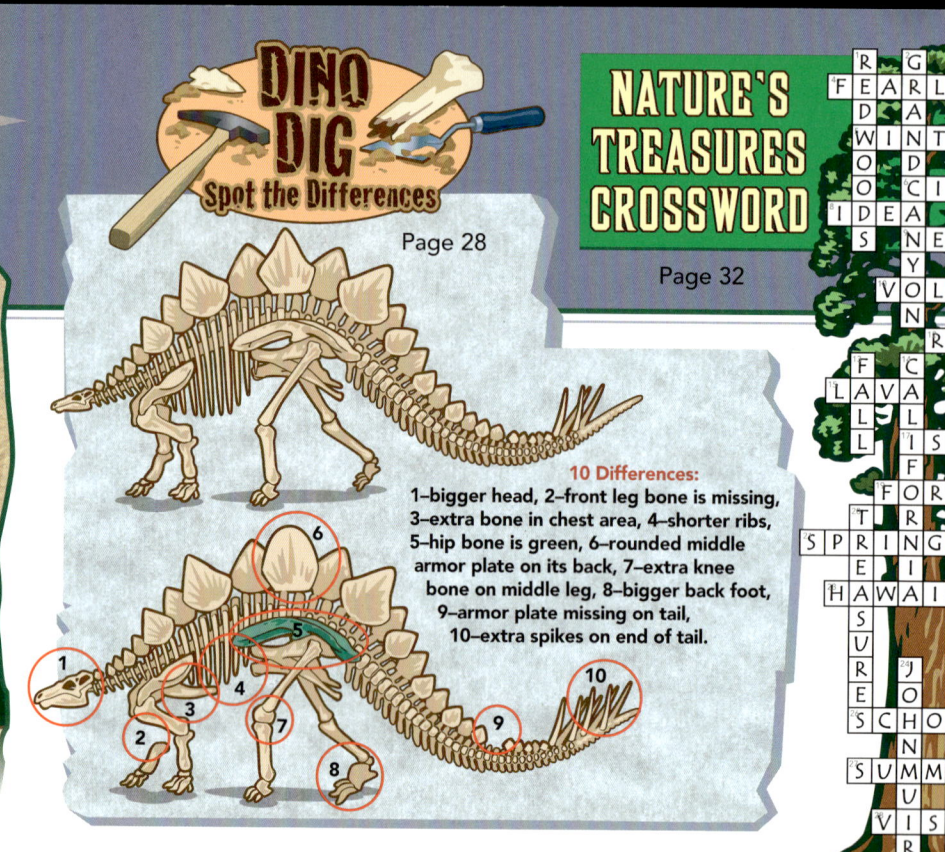

10 Differences:
1–bigger head, 2–front leg bone is missing, 3–extra bone in chest area, 4–shorter ribs, 5–hip bone is green, 6–rounded middle armor plate on its back, 7–extra knee bone on middle leg, 8–bigger back foot, 9–armor plate missing on tail, 10–extra spikes on end of tail.

Nature's Treasures Crossword
Page 32

Across/Down answers shown: FEARLESS, DESERT, RED, GRAND, WOODS, WINTER, CITIES, IDEA, CANYON, SEASONS, NEVADA, SPRING, VOLCANO, RAINS, FALL, CALIFORNIA, ROCK, LAVA, ISLAND, FOREST, NATURE, TREES, HAWAII, HIKE, JOHN, MUIR, SCHOOL, YOSEMITE, SUMMER, VISIT

Search for Wildlife
Page 30

Grand Canyon Maze
Page 34

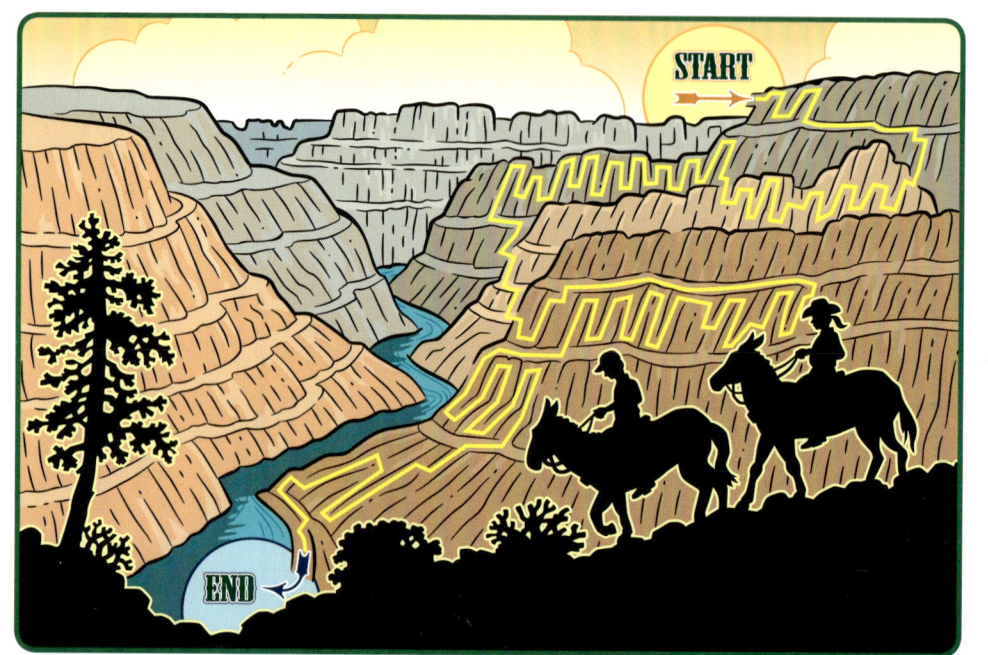

Activity Checklist
Page 39

- HIKING
- CANOEING ✗
- HORSEBACK RIDING ✗
- SWIMMING
- BIKING
- CAMPING
- PICNICKING ✗
- SKIING ✗
- ICE-SKATING

48